Frederick Milnes Edge

Slavery Doomed

Or, the contest between free and slave labour in the United States

Frederick Milnes Edge

Slavery Doomed
Or, the contest between free and slave labour in the United States

ISBN/EAN: 9783337393274

Printed in Europe, USA, Canada, Australia, Japan

Cover: Foto ©ninafisch / pixelio.de

More available books at **www.hansebooks.com**

SLAVERY DOOMED:

OR,

THE CONTEST BETWEEN

FREE AND SLAVE LABOUR

IN

THE UNITED STATES.

BY

FREDERICK MILNES EDGE.

LONDON:

SMITH, ELDER AND CO., 65, CORNHILL.

———

M.DCCC.LX.

TO

THE RIGHT HON. HENRY LORD BROUGHAM,

THE LONG-TRIED, PERSEVERING, AND FAITHFUL FRIEND

OF

HIS COUNTRY AND MANKIND,

𝕿𝖍𝖎𝖘 𝖂𝖔𝖗𝖐 𝖎𝖘 𝖉𝖊𝖉𝖎𝖈𝖆𝖙𝖊𝖉,

WITH SENTIMENTS OF PROFOUND ESTEEM,

BY

THE AUTHOR.

PREFACE.

The Author of this work has enjoyed peculiar advantages for the study of the important issues now agitating the United States. A resident during five years in that country, he witnessed many of the occurrences herein related, while professional duties in connection with the press, during the last Presidential election, introduced him, as it were, behind the scenes, and afforded him the opportunity of becoming personally acquainted with many of the leaders of opinion in the American Republic.

Englishmen and Europeans generally have, hitherto, felt little interest with regard to trans-Atlantic concerns. Now, however, that the state of American politics is likely to seriously and immediately affect ourselves, a general desire is arising to obtain increased information upon a subject fraught with so much importance to the manufactures and commerce of the world at large, and involving the destinies of a race which the white man has held in bondage, in defiance of the Almighty's laws and the dictates of political economy.

That the facts contained in this volume may arrest the attention of philanthropists and statesmen, and secure the sympathy of Englishmen for the free citizens of America, in their noble efforts to limit, and eventually destroy, that "peculiar Institution" which has so long oppressed themselves, and degraded millions of their fellow-creatures, is the ardent prayer of

THE AUTHOR.

London, May, 1860.

INTRODUCTION.

DURING the past two years, we imported from the United States the following quantities of their great staple, COTTON :—

1858.	1859.
7,439,623 cwts.	8,586,672 cwts.

From all other sources, during the same periods, the amounts were as follow :—

1858.	1859.
1,795,575 cwts.	2,359,659 cwts.

We are thus mainly dependent upon the United States for the raw material of England's greatest manufacture. Cotton is king in commerce, and commerce and manufactures have placed Great Britain where she is. Stop her cotton supply, and you hurl her from her rank amidst the nations.

THAT SUPPLY, SO FAR AS IT DEPENDS UPON THE UNITED STATES, IS NOW IN PERIL.

If a question arise in any part of Europe or Asia, involving the conquest or annexation of some petty principality, Great Britain immediately becomes vitally interested. Debate follows upon debate in Parliament, and our press seems to have room for nought but extravagant amplification of the subject. Territories far distant, barren, and thinly peopled, are invested with ridiculous importance, whereas that immense Republic beyond the Atlantic is a sealed book to us, although the source, mainstay, and support of England's prosperity.

We know that the United States furnish us with cotton, tobacco, rice, wheat, corn, hemp, flax, &c., and we imagine they will necessarily continue to furnish us with those products until the end of time; but we know nothing of the impending crisis in that country, and ignore the storm which is ready to burst.

This year, the United States elect a President in the place of Mr. Buchanan. For the first time in the history of the Republic, the two principles of Free and Slave labour stand face to face. The Northern Free States are preparing to declare that Slavery is *sectional,* and shall henceforward be illegal, except in those States where it already exists. The South is preparing to maintain that Slavery is

*national—first, at the polls, and afterwards, by dis-
union or civil war.*

The Republican, or Free State party, has now the
majority sufficient to elect a chief magistrate of the
Republic. The President elected must swear to
maintain the union of the States at any and all
hazards, and the majority will force him to keep his
oath. With civil war impending, with the Southern ports perhaps blockaded, and all communication
with the North destroyed, how shall we obtain our
cotton?

But there are great and holy principles at issue in
the present contest, which must interest the lovers
of liberty throughout the world. When England
emancipated the Slaves in her colonies, the Slaveholders were a small and unimportant body of men,
compared with the entire British people. In the
United States the question assumes a widely different
aspect; for since the establishment of the Republic
the government of the Confederation has been directed
by the Slaveholding oligarchs, who are still supreme
in the Capitol. The hour of their fall draws nigh,
and the blow comes not from without, but from the
free men of the Northern States, who are preparing

to declare that " Come what will, Slavery shall be restrained."

The issue is so tremendous, and the climax so near, that it is worth our while, as Englishmen, to examine the question closely.

CONTENTS.

xiv CONTENTS.

SLAVERY DOOMED.

ESTABLISHMENT OF THE UNION.

The internal political affairs of the United States
of North America are so little understood in this
country, that we are compelled to go back to the
very establishment of the Republic, in order to obtain
a just appreciation of the principles at work. The
thirteen States which originally formed the Union
lay in different latitudes, and their products were
consequently different. To England's disgrace,
African slavery had been forced upon them when
colonies; but negro labour quickly succumbed to the
white man in the white man's climate of the north.
The country became divided into two sections—the
Farm, and the Plantation : in the former, the Caucasian braved the snows of an almost Arctic winter;
in the latter, the African toiled and sang beneath a

1

torrid sun. But when these colonies united in one
common aim of independence, and resolved to form a
separate and distinct nation and government, it was
necessary to balance their diverse interests. The
fathers of the Republic effected this in the only
manner possible. The Constitution of the United
States provided that where Slavery already existed—
where it had been forced upon them by the mother
country, and still lived—it should not be interfered
with. But in process of years the far-spreading territory of the Republic became peopled with the white
man. New communities formed, and applied for
admission into the Confederation; and the question
presented itself of the extension or non-extension
of Slavery. The original compromise necessitated
further compromises, and what was at first a social
accident resolved itself eventually into a means of
political domination.

In order to balance the power of the Free States
with that of the Slave, the authors of the Constitution
had given the white men of the latter an additional
vote, equal to three-fifths of their negroes. But in
process of time, immigration caused the Northern
States to increase in an unexpected ratio, and the
balance of power became destroyed. Then commenced the struggle which is still pending—that

"irrepressible conflict" between serfdom and freedom which can only be decided one way, and which will be determined, in all human probability, within a few years.

THE NORTHERN STATES NOT ABOLITIONIST.

It is necessary that Europeans should understand that the issue pending between the Free and the Slave States is not one of the abolition, but of the extension or non-extension of Slavery. The thirteen States which originally formed the Union, agreed to a constitution which prevented negro vassalage being interfered with in those portions of the Confederation where it then existed; and every succeeding State on entering the Union bound itself not to meddle with the internal affairs of any other State. To all intents and purposes, except that of mutual defence against foreign aggression, the various States of the North American Confederation are as separate and distinct sovereignties as Austria and Prussia. Thus, for example, a murderer in the State of New York cannot be seized in New Jersey, or any other State, except upon requisition of the governor of the former to that of the latter, who causes the offender to be arrested by his own officers, and delivers him across the frontier to the authorities of the State where the crime was committed. Slavery is a *State,* not a *Federal,* institution, and it must therefore be understood that *Slavery can only be abolished by the Legislature of the State where it exists.* What the Free North is labouring to effect is, to prevent the legalization, and, consequently, the existence of Slavery in the wide-spreading territories of the Republic not yet sufficiently peopled to form into States. In effecting this—in declaring that henceforth and for evermore Slavery shall no further extend within the Republic—the accursed system of African serfdom will eventually die out—become, in fact, stifled by the freedom surrounding it. Only so far is the Republican, or Free State party, Abolitionist.

It is necessary that this position be clearly understood, for there are certain individuals in the United States whose views and aims are of the most ultra-Abolitionist character, and whose writings are well and favourably known in Europe. The Republican party, whilst endorsing all their remarks upon the moral aspect of the question—what, in America, is called " the higher law "—declares that the abolition of Slavery in any State or States by federal authority is not their object, because *not within their province or power.*

Mr. Chase, the Governor of the State of Ohio, thus defined the policy of the Free State party in November last :—

" Let us not be told that in thus maintaining the rights and interests of free labour, we act an unfriendly part to our fellow citizens of the Slave States. It is not so. We propose no interference with them or with their Slavery. So far as we are concerned, they and their States shall have every right which the Constitution gives them. I have always said so. I never refused to measures for the promotion of the interests of citizens of the Slave States as cordial support as I have given to like measures for the benefit of my own. We wage no war with any section of our common country. We insist only that the few shall not be permitted to control the many—that the government of the people shall be in the hands of the people, and not in the hands of a privileged class—that the slave-holders of the Slave States shall not force their Slavery either into the Free States or the free territories of the Republic."

Mr. Seward, the acknowledged leader of the Republican party, thus declared its object to the assembled Senate of the United States on the 29th of February :—

" The choice of the nation is now between the Democratic party and the Republican party. Its principles (the Republican party's) and policy are, therefore, justly and even necessarily examined. I know of only one policy which it has adopted or avowed, namely:—*The saving of the territories of the United States, if possible, by constitutional and lawful means, from being homes for Slavery and Polygamy.* Who, that considers where this nation exists, of what races it is composed, in what age of the world it acts its part on the public stage, and what are its predominant institutions, customs, habits, and sentiments, doubts that the Republican party can and will, if unwaveringly faithful to that policy, and just and loyal in all beside, carry it into triumphal success? To doubt, is to be uncertain whether civilization can improve or Christianity save mankind."

It is a strange, though perhaps an easily explained fact, that Slavery opponents from the Slave States are thorough Abolitionists, not confining themselves to the strictly conservative and legal policy of the Northern, or Republican party. The former are brought into contact with Slavery itself in all its daily horrors, and therefore desire its annihilation *in* their own State. The latter are only acquainted with it in its efforts to extend itself into, at present, Free territory, and, therefore, do not oppose aught but the extension. We, in Europe, have some difficulty in justly appreciating the difference, and recognizing only two principles, two phases of the question,— Slavery or Abolition; we applaud the reasonings of such persons as Gerritt Smith, Frederick Douglass, and Mrs. Stowe. But their ideas have no influence upon public movements in the United States; and have as much connection with the aims of the Free State party as manhood suffrage with Lord John Russell's new Reform Bill.

A work has lately appeared in America entitled, *The Impending Crisis of the South, and how to meet it.* The author, *Hinton Rowan Helper*, is a citizen of the Slave State, North Carolina, and he proves conclusively that the "peculiar institution" is ruining the southern portion of the Confederation. But he does not confine himself to argument and statistics; he launches forth into fierce denunciation of the Slave-holding oligarchy, and addresses them in such violent language as the following:—

"Frown, sirs, fret, foam, prepare your weapons, threat, strike, shoot, stab, bring on civil war, dissolve the Union, nay, annihilate the solar system if you will—do all this, more, less, better, worse, anything—do what you will, sirs, you can neither foil nor intimidate us ; our purpose is as firmly fixed as the eternal pillars of Heaven ; we have determined to abolish Slavery, and, so help us, God, abolish it we will ! "

This certainly exceeds in violence anything which has hitherto come from American Abolitionists, and would lead some to suppose that the author has been in servitude himself. Mr. Hinton, however, is a white man, and writes not more from opposition to Slavery, as a moral wrong, than from conviction of the injury it is doing his native State.

Such works as this *Impending Crisis of the South* and *Uncle Tom's Cabin* are read and generally approved in the northern portion of the Union, but have little or no effect upon the political action of that section. Their influence may be summed up in the remarks of Thomas Jefferson to Dr. Price, upon his treatise, *Emancipation in America* :—

"Southward of the Chesapeake, your book will find but few readers concurring with it in sentiment on the subject of Slavery. From the mouth to the head of the Chesapeake, the bulk of the people will approve it in theory, and it will find a respectable minority ready to adopt it in practice; a minority, which, for weight, and worth of character, preponderates against the greater number who have not the courage to divest their families of a property which, however, keeps their consciences unquiet. Northward of the Chesapeake you may find here and there an opponent to your doctrine, as you may find here and there a robber or a murderer; but in no great number." * * *
" This [Virginia] is the next State to which we may turn our eyes for the interesting spectacle of justice in conflict with avarice and oppression—a conflict where the sacred side is gaining daily new recruits from the influx into office of young men, grown and growing up." * *

"Be not, then, discouraged. What you have written will do a great deal of good; and could you still trouble yourself about our welfare, no man is more able to help the labouring side."

REASONS WHY SLAVERY HAS BEEN ABOLISHED IN SOME STATES AND RETAINED IN OTHERS.

When the North American colonies resolved upon independence of the mother country, and victory had crowned their efforts, they found much difficulty in agreeing upon such a Federal Constitution as would not interfere with conflicting rights and interests. Slavery had existed in each and every of those colonies, but in some it had been abolished.

Although Slavery had thus been got rid of in the *North*, and retained in the South, we must not look for the reason of that abolition or retention in geographical and climatial causes alone. *In no portion of the United States is the weather too hot for white men to labour in the open air*, and there is no occupation in which the African race is employed —from Virginia to Florida—which the Caucasian cannot equally perform. The cultivation of cotton, the main staple of the South, is one of the least laborious in agriculture; so much so that our West Indian planters are opposed to its introduction into

Jamaica and other islands, knowing that it will draw off their hands from the cultivation of sugar. In the southernmost portions of the Union, railroad and other engineering works are carried on mainly by white men, and this labour is infinitely more trying than that of agriculture. Yet, if we examine the rates of mortality in the different States (not merely during a single year, which might be an exceptional one, but over a decennial period), we find that the ratio of mortality amongst the whites is considerably higher in the northern than in the southern portions of the country. This assertion may appear extraordinary, considering that the diseases of the South belong to a latitude foreign to the white man; but we have the authority of the United States Census Returns for the statement.

We must look for the causes of the early abolition of Slavery in the North to religion alone. The colonists who settled in the northern portions of the British possessions were the Puritans — men driven from England by ecclesiastical tyranny, and seeking religious liberty as much, if not more, than civil. These men settled in the now States of Massachusetts, New Hampshire, Connecticut, and Rhode Island, and formed their constitutions and made their laws out of the Bible. If we examine the

records of the above-mentioned colonies, we find that
the Scriptures were, literally, the constant companion
of the settlers, and their rule of life and government. True it is that their Christianity took a strong
ascetic turn, a dispensation half way between the
Old and New Testaments; but they were honest in
their convictions, and quickly found out that Slavery
was not consonant with the teachings of Christ. New
York and New Jersey, colonized in the first instance
by the Bible-reading, Lutheran Dutch, and subsequently reduced beneath English sway, underwent
similar changes and from similar reasons; whilst the
descendants of Penn and the Quakers could not long
retain an institution so repugnant to the principles of
their creed.

Turn we now to the South, and we shall find a
different civilization obtaining, and widely different
principles at work. Virginia and North Carolina
were colonized by the Cavaliers, men who answered
the psalms of the Puritans by the songs of the Stuart
court. Feudal lords or retainers in their forsaken
country, they naturally sought to form around them
a similar civilization in their adopted home. The
English " Estate" emigrated, and became the American " Plantation." Serfs were changed for negro
slaves. The same holds good with reference to

Maryland, settled by Irish Catholics, and the Huguenot colony of South Carolina, which grew out of a strictly Feudal element. Georgia, colonized at a later period than the above, under the auspices of General Oglethorpe, adopted similar usages to Virginia and the Carolinas, on the ground that as the agricultural productions of their settlement were the same, so must their mode of cultivation be. Seeing no other excuse for Slave-holding, it was a plausible defence of their iniquity to assert that agricultural operations could only be carried on in southern climes by African labour, and that as the negro was incapable of taking care of himself, his master should do so by making him his chattel. The world keeps moving, and so do the Southern States of the American Union, though it be, like a crab—backwards. Slavery, which they originally defended, on the ground of their own self-interest, they now advocate on holy and Christian principles, teaching "a new gospel than that delivered to the saints," and declaring that by its means "the children of Ham will be brought into the fold of Christ." And there are thousands of misguided men in the South who honestly believe they are doing God service in thus acting. Truly the human heart is the devil's lawyer.

After the North American colonies had freed themselves from British rule, a certain period elapsed during which the new Republic found itself in want of that autonomy which a Constitution alone could give. The making a Constitution for a new people is one of the most difficult operations which any man, or body of men, can undertake; especially in this instance, where the antagonistic principles of free and slave labour were to be made to act in unison. In reference to this difficulty, Senator Seward gives the following testimony:—

" The fathers of the Republic encountered it. They even adjusted it so that it might have given us much less than our present disquiet, had not circumstances afterwards occurred which they, wise as they were, had not clearly foreseen. Although they had inherited, yet they generally condemned, the practice of Slavery, and hoped for its discontinuance. They expressed this when they asserted, in the Declaration of Independence, as a fundamental principle of American society, that all men are created equal, and have inalienable rights to life, liberty, and the pursuit of happiness. Each State, however, reserved to itself exclusive political power over the subject of Slavery, within its own borders. Nevertheless, it unavoidably presented itself in the consultations on a bond of federal union. The new government was to be a representative one. Slaves were capital in some States, in others, capital had no investments in labour. Should those Slaves be represented as

capital or as persons, taxed as capital or as persons, or
should they not be represented or taxed at all? The fathers
disagreed, debated long, and compromised at last. Each
State, they determined, shall have two senators in Congress. Three-fifths of the Slaves shall be elsewhere represented, and be taxed as persons. What should be done if
the Slave should escape into a labour State? Should that
State confess him to be a chattel, and restore him as such,
or might it regard him as a person, and harbour and protect him as a man? They compromised again, and decided that no person held to labour or service in one State,
by the laws thereof, shall, by any law or regulation of that
State, be discharged from such labour or service, but shall
be delivered up on claim to the person to whom such
labour or service shall be due."

It was not long before these two principles of
free and slave labour came into fierce and often-
recurring antagonism; but we shall leave this question of Slavery aggression to a later period, and
proceed to compare the relative positions of the
Northern and Southern States at the outset of their
career, and the progress they have respectively made
in social and political well-being.

COMPARISON OF THE FREE AND SLAVE STATES.

At the period of the adoption of the Constitution, the territory occupied by the Southern States was about of equal extent to that of the Northern. It would seem as though the two sections prepared themselves for rivalry in the race of civilization by equalizing their several chances; for as their respective territories were equal, so was their population. Each numbered two millions, including 500,000 slaves in the South. Nor did commerce show partiality for either, since the returns of 1793 report 2,058,113*l.* of Northern exports to 1,932,105*l.* Southern. The assessment for direct taxes, made a few years subsequently (1799), continued this parallel of equality, there being to the value of 84,000,000*l.* in each section. From 1795 to 1816, the South took the lead in commerce by about one million sterling annually; whilst the North manufactured forty million yards per annum of woollen, cotton, and linen fabrics to thirty-four millions of the South. Population and property at this period (1816) stood as follow :—

	South.	North.
Population . . .	2,749,795*	4,326,550
Property . .	£180,510,685	£218,984,274

* Exclusive of Slaves.

Forty years have worked an amazing change upon
the commercial prospects of the two rivals. New
York, under the beneficent influence of free institutions, now stands the peer of London and Liverpool,
and Philadelphia, Boston, and other northern ports
follow closely in her wake. What remains of
Charleston, Mobile, and other southern harbours
more than the recollection of their former prosperity?
New Orleans is, for the present, an exception to the
rule: commanding as it does the commerce of the
great valley of the Mississippi, the cotton planters
naturally avail themselves of that immense stream to
forward their staple to market. But when the railroad system is complete throughout the Southern
States, the traffic will be diverted to the port of
New York, not merely from the fact of water-carriage
never successfully competing (even in America) with
railroads, but because that city is so much nearer
Liverpool. Liverpool is the destination of nearly all
the cotton grown in the United States, and it is the
condition of the market on the banks of the Mersey
which fixes the price of the staple at the mouth of
the Mississippi.

It would appear as though an all-wise Providence
had set apart the American Continent for the arena
in which the principles of right and might, of slavery

and freedom, should battle out their claims on their own merits. We may take the two States of New York and Virginia as champions of the respective interests. They were so formerly and are so now. Each contains the greatest number of white inhabitants in its section, and of all Slave States, Virginia possesses the greatest number of Slaves. She calls herself, " the Old Dominion," " the Mother of Presidents," while her rival is known as " the Empire State." Mr. Helper, in his work, *The Impending Crisis of the South*, thus compares them :—

NEW YORK AND VIRGINIA.

" In 1790, when the first census was taken, New York contained 340,120 inhabitants ; at the same time the population of Virginia was 748,308, being more than twice the number of New York. Just sixty years afterward, as we learn from the census of 1850, New York had a population of 3,097,394 ; while that of Virginia was only 1,421,661, being less than half the number of New York ! In 1791, the exports of New York amounted to 2,505,465 dols.; the exports of Virginia amounted to 3,130,865 dols. In 1852, the exports of New York amounted to 87,484,456 dols.; the exports of Virginia, during the same year, amounted to only 2,724,657 dols. In 1790, the imports of New York and Virginia were about equal ; in 1853, the imports of New York amounted

2

to the enormous sum of 178,270,999 dols.; while those of Virginia, for the same period, amounted to the pitiful sum of only 399,004 dols. In 1850, the products of manufactures, mining and the mechanic arts in New York amounted to 237,597,249 dols.; those of Virginia amounted to only 29,705,387 dols. At the taking of the last census, the value of real and personal property in Virginia, including negroes, was 391,646,438 dols.; that of New York, exclusive of any monetary valuation of human beings, was 1,080,309,216 dols. In August, 1856, the real and personal estate assessed in the city of New York amounted in valuation to 511,740,491 dols., showing that *New York City alone is worth far more than the whole State of Virginia.*"

In the comparison we are about to institute of the Free and Slave States, it is necessary to bear continually in mind that the two sections of the Republic started with equal promise of advancement, and that if either were more favoured than the other, it was the southern. Less rigorous winters, more fruitful soil, a better supply of wood and water in the latter, would naturally offer inducements to settlers. If these inducements have not sufficed, there can be but one explanation, namely, the institution of Slavery. We, in this part of the world, little know the influence of the system as it obtains in the Southern States of the American Union. It acts as an insurmountable obstacle to immigration, and drives thousands from the home of their fathers. Our "cold shade of the aristocracy" is warm and genial in comparison with its icy teachings, for the position is openly taken that "labour is a badge of servitude." The hundreds of thousands of emigrants who have quitted Europe during the past ten or fifteen years, quickly discovered that the Slave districts offered no homes to them, for whilst they were regarded as on a *moral* par with the Slaves, being obliged to work to eat, they were undersold, so to speak, by the latter. The "Chattels" are instructed in all branches of trade, and are let out by their masters at comparatively nominal prices; far too moderate for the poor white man to feed, clothe, and lodge his family upon. In a new country, immigration is the first requirement, the first sign of advancement; and we need no better proof of the evils which have befallen the South from the "peculiar institution" than its rendering immigration impossible.

The following tables give the population of the various States in 1840 and 1850, and the estimated numbers in 1860 :—

POPULATION OF THE UNITED STATES.

SLAVE STATES, 1840.

States.	Whites.	Slaves.	Free Coloured.
Alabama	335,185	253,532	2,039
Arkansas	77,174	19,935	465
Delaware	58,561	2,605	16,919
Florida...................	27,943	25,717	817
Georgia	407,695	280,944	2,753
Kentucky...............	590,253	182,258	7,317
Louisiana...............	158,457	168,452	25,502
Maryland...............	318,204	89,737	62,078
Mississippi	179,074	195,211	1,366
Missouri	323,888	58,240	1,574
North Carolina.........	484,870	245,817	22,732
South Carolina.........	259,084	327,038	8,276
Tennessee...............	640,627	183,059	5,524
Texas	Not yet in the Confederation.		
Virginia	740,858	449,087	49,852
District of Columbia...	30,657	4,694	8,361
Total...........	4,632,530	2,486,326	215,575

SLAVE STATES, 1850.

States.	Whites.	Slaves.	Free Coloured.
Alabama	426,514	342,844	2,265
Arkansas	162,189	47,100	608
Delaware	71,169	2,290	18,073
Florida..................	47,203	39,310	932
Georgia	521,572	381,682	2,931
Kentucky...............	761,413	210,981	10,011
Louisiana............	255,491	244,809	17,462
Maryland	417,943	90,368	74,723
Mississippi	295,718	309,878	930
Missouri	592,004	87,422	2,618
North Carolina.........	553,028	288,548	27,463
South Carolina.........	274,563	384,984	8,960
Tennessee...............	756,836	239,459	6,422
Texas	154,034	58,161	397
Virginia	894,800	472,528	54,333
District of Columbia...	37,941	3,687	10,059
Total............	6,222,418	3,204,051	238,187

PROBABLE POPULATION IN 1860.

SLAVE STATES.

States.	Whites.	Slaves.	Free Coloured.
Alabama	507,139	409,695	2,684
Arkansas	274,570	96,111	787
Delaware	82,428	2,498	19,849
Florida	56,165	46,975	1,104
Georgia	577,373	446,546	3,334
Kentucky	946,065	230,229	10,995
Louisiana	333,815	311,175	18,244
Maryland	519,300	98,612	82,069
Mississippi	351,864	369,703	1,102
Missouri	735,573	95,397	2,875
North Carolina.........	658,028	344,812	32,554
South Carolina.........	326,692	460,052	10,621
Tennessee...............	900,531	286,150	7,612
Texas	260,764	118,672	514
Virginia	1,111,800	515,636	59,675
District of Columbia...	46,956	2,896	12,102
Total............	7,689,063	3,835,159	266,121

FREE STATES.

States.	1840.*	1850.*	1860.
California	Not settled.	92,597	700,000
Connecticut	309,978	370,792	480,710
Illinois	476,183	851,470	1,995,719
Indiana...............	685,866	988,416	2,316,699
Iowa....................	43,112	192,214	723,328
Maine	501,793	583,169	756,044
Massachusetts	737,699	994,514	1,289,330
Michigan	212,267	397,654	746,829
New Hampshire ...	284,574	317,976	412,237
New Jersey	373,306	489,555	613,082
New York	2,428,921	3,097,394	3,878,945
Ohio..................	1,519,467	1,980,329	2,479,966
Pennsylvania	1,724,033	2,311,786	2,895,106
Rhode Island	108,830	147,545	191,283
Vermont	291,948	314,120	407,238
Wisconsin............	30,945	305,391	999,381
Minnesota............	Not settled.	6,077†	200,000
Oregon	Not settled.	13,294†	150,000
Total............	9,728,922	13,454,293	21,235,897

* Sixth and seventh census of the United States (official returns).
† Then only territories.

It is a somewhat difficult task to make even a tolerably correct estimate of the increase of population in the United States, immigration being so capricious. Thus, there arrived in the port of New York, during the year 1858, 78,589 emigrants, a sad falling off from the numbers of the preceding year, 183,775.* We shall not receive the official report of the eighth census of the United States (taken this year) until 1862 or 1863; but our estimate will not prove wide of the mark. Certain of the States take a census every four or five years, independently of the federal one, and we are thus enabled to judge with some accuracy of the numbers in 1860. Our task is not difficult with regard to the Slave section, for the ratio is comparatively moderate and regular. The census of the Slave State of Alabama in 1855, gave the following result :—

Whites.	Slaves.	Free Negroes.
464,920	374,782	2,466

Thus we have a ratio of increase per cent. per annum, during five years, as follows :—

Whites.	Slaves.	Free Negroes.
1·75	1·79	1·71

Whence we deduce the results given in the table above. The States of Florida, Mississippi, North

* Reports of New York Commissioners of Emigration.

and South Carolina, and Tennessee, only number their people every ten years; but as those States are subject to the same influences as Alabama, we may judge of their increase, since 1850, by the decennial ratio of the latter, viz.—

Whites.	Slaves.	Free Negroes.
18·98	19·41	18·53

The census of Arkansas, in 1858, gave the following result :—

Whites.	Slaves.	Free Negroes.
247,131	83,334	748

The annual ratio during eight years being—

Whites.	Slaves.	Free Negroes.
5·40	7·39	2·62

We take this result, an extraordinary one for a southern State, as a guide to find the population of Texas, the decennial ratio being—

Whites.	Slaves.	Free Negroes.
69·29	104·04	29·57

Texas and Arkansas lie in the south-west, and are comparatively unsettled. The great increase is caused by planters moving into them from the older southern States, not by foreign immigration or disregard of the Malthusian theory.

The State of Georgia census last year (1859) gave this result:—

Whites.	Slaves.	Free Negroes.
571,534	439,592	3,292

And the annual percentage of increase—

Whites.	Slaves.	Free Negroes.
1·02	1·58	1·30

The ratio of Florida, as to all three classes of the population, is about the same as that of Georgia; in classing it with Alabama we advantage it.

Louisiana, by her State census, also taken last year, shows the following population:—

Whites.	Slaves.	Free Negroes.
325,007	303,800	18,164

The decennial ratio of increase being—

Whites.	Slaves.	Free Negroes.
30·65	27·11	4·43

This is the only Slave State which increases its population by foreign immigrants, the nationalities being mostly French, Spanish, and the southern races generally. It may almost be regarded as a French settlement. The heightened slave ratio has not the same connection with the white population as in the other States, but is due mainly to the fact that New Orleans is the great African mart. Planters from the cotton, sugar, and rice districts there purchase and sell their human "property," and it is for this market that Virginia breeds or "raises" a large proportion of her negroes. Droves of these unfortunates are kept on hand in New Orleans waiting favourable turns of the market.

The report of the Auditor of Public Accounts of Virginia gives the population of his State in 1859, as follows:—

Whites.	Slaves.	Free Negroes.
1,087,918	511,154	59,118

Comparing this result with the census of 1850, we have this ratio for ten years:—

Whites.	Slaves.	Free Negroes.
24·25	9·12	9·83

This State is divided into two districts, the Eastern and the Western. In the latter, the population is almost entirely white, and the political sentiment is strongly adverse to Slave labour; the Abolition element, in fact, is becoming most powerful, and attracts, in consequence, immigrants from other southern States.

Delaware, Kentucky, Maryland, and Missouri, lying contiguous to the Free States, are fast losing their pro-Slavery character; and we have, therefore, judged their present population upon the ratio of

Virginia. The proportion of Slaves in Delaware and Maryland is yearly diminishing, while the number of free negroes is increasing; and the time is not far distant when these two States will abolish human servitude. Missouri, in the far west, is approaching that desired result in a still more rapid manner; but this fact her returns do not sufficiently indicate. In the opinion of many American statesmen, five years hence will see her a Free State.

[The district of Columbia is a small territory set apart for federal purposes, and is governed directly by Congress, the idea being that it is the joint property of all the States. We are obliged to judge of its present population by the returns of 1840 and 1850, as it is unaffected by causes which influence other portions of the Confederation.]

The estimated population of California, in 1856, was 507,067, showing a ratio of *annual* increase, since 1850, of 32·76. During these six years, however, the immigration had been enormous, consequent upon the gold discoveries; but the excitement must have cooled down since, or have been drawn off in the direction of Australia, Sonora, Fraser River, &c. We have, therefore, put the population in round numbers at 700,000, though that may be under the mark.

Illinois, by its census of 1855, gave 1,306,576 inhabitants,—a clear gain of 455,106 in five years, almost all immigration. These Western States are drawing off the surplus population of the world: the ratio is 8·89 per annum, or 134·39 in ten years. We have placed the sister State of Indiana in the same category.

Iowa State census of last year gives her population as 633,549—a decennial rate of increase of 276·32.

Massachusetts State census in 1855 gives the number of inhabitants at 1,132,369. Annual ratio 2·63, decennial 29·64, upon which we may estimate the populations of the other New England States— Connecticut, Maine, New Hampshire, Rhode Island, and Vermont. These States are not subject to immigration to such a degree as the Western, being, like New York, New Jersey, Pennsylvania, and Ohio, thickly settled, and the land consequently more valuable.

The census of Michigan, in 1854, gave 511,672 inhabitants, a decennial ratio of 87·81.

The census returns of New York State, in 1855, showed 3,466,212, or a decennial ratio of 25·23. We are thus enabled to judge of the populations of Ohio, Pennsylvania, and New Jersey.

Wisconsin, in 1855, numbered 552,451 inhabitants, showing an annual ratio of 12·58, or of 227·24 in ten years.

Minnesota is estimated to have the above population at the present time. In May, 1858, it was 150,042.

Oregon, the youngest of the States, is fast becoming settled. Three years ago, her inhabitants numbered upwards of 43,000; at the present time, her population is considered to be in the neighbourhood of 150,000.

ACRES UNDER CULTIVATION IN 1850 AND 1860.

SLAVE STATES.

States.	Area.	Under Cultivation in 1850.*	Under Cultivation in 1860.†
	Acres.	Acres.	Acres.
Alabama	32,462,080	4,435,614	5,277,490
Arkansas	33,406,720	781,530	1,323,100
Delaware	1,356,000	580,862	721,721
Florida	37,931,520	349,049	415,300
Georgia	37,120,000	6,378,479	7,060,900
Kentucky	24,115,200	5,968,270	7,415,590
Louisiana	29,715,840	1,590,025	2,072,590
Maryland	5,987,840	2,797,905	3,476,390
Mississippi	30,179,840	3,444,358	4,098,100
Missouri	43,123,200	2,938,425	3,650,989
North Carolina	28,800,000	5,453,975	6,489,140
South Carolina	15,680,000	4,072,651	4,845,173
Tennessee	29,184,000	5,175,173	6,157,423
Texas	151,885,440	639,117	1,081,960
Virginia	39,265,280	10,360,135	12,872,467
District of Columbia	32,000	16,267	20,132
Total	540,244,960	54,981,835	66,978,465

* The seventh census of the United States (official report).

† Calculated upon the increase of white population in each State during the preceding ten years.

FREE STATES.

States.	Area.	Under Cultivation in 1850.*	Under Cultivation in 1860.†
	Acres.	Acres.	Acres.
California	120,000,000	32,454	‡700,000
Connecticut	2,991,360	1,768,178	2,292,266
Illinois	35,459,200	5,039,545	11,812,832
Indiana	21,637,760	5,046,543	11,828,598
Iowa	32,584,960	824,682	3,103,443
Maine	19,200,000	2,039,596	2,644,137
Massachusetts	4,992,000	2,133,436	2,766,788
Michigan	35,595,520	1,929,110	3,623,061
New Hampshire	5,939,200	2,251,488	2,918,829
New Jersey	5,324,800	1,767,991	2,214,066
New York	29,440,000	12,408,964	15,539,741
Ohio	25,576,960	9,851,493	12,337,025
Pennsylvania	29,440,000	8,628,619	10,805,616
Rhode Island	835,840	356,487	462,149
Vermont	6,535,680	2,601,409	3,372,466
Wisconsin	34,511,360	1,045,499	3,421,294
Minnesota	106,240,000	5,035§	1,500,000
Oregon	118,419,200	132,857§	1,200,000
Total	634,723,840	57,683,386	92,542,311

* The seventh census of the United States (official report).
† Calculated upon the increase of white population in each State during the preceding ten years.
‡ There were 508,267 acres under cultivation, in 1857.
§ Then only territories.

In comparing the number of acres under cultivation in the Northern and Southern States, it is necessary to understand that the system in either is totally dissimilar. *The staples of the South are grown, not cultivated,* and the land thus becomes quickly exhausted. Whole districts, which formerly were covered with plantations, now lie in dreary waste, the very ground blasted. The Slave-holders, of course, declare that cotton, tobacco, &c. exhaust the soil, and that they are necessitated to move to virgin land ; ignoring the fact that, at some future period, their entire territory may become occupied. In the North, the system is widely different, being similar to our own.

PRODUCE OF THE TWO SECTIONS, 1850.

Produce.	Total, Free States.	Total, Slave States.
	Bushels.	Bushels.
Barley	5,002,013	161,907
Beans and Pease............	1,542,295	7,637,227
Buckwheat	8,550,245	405,357
Clover and Grass Seed......	762,265	123,517
Flax Seed..................	358,923	203,484
Indian Corn	242,618,650	348,992,282
Oats	96,590,371	49,882,799
Potatoes	59,033,170·	44,847,420
Rye	12,574,623	1,608,240
Wheat	72,157,486	27,904,476
Total..................	499,190,041	481,766,709

PRODUCE OF THE TWO SECTIONS—*continued.*

Produce.	Total, Free States.	Total, Slave States.
	Cwts.	Cwts.
Beeswax and Honey.........	61,503	71,114
Butter and Cheese...........	3,123,757	612,805
Flax	27,216	42,555
Hay	253,819,640	22,755,680
Hemp	3,960	693,460
Hops...........................	30,921	301
Maple Sugar..................	287,158	18,649
Tobacco.......................	131,715	1,651,999
Wool	353,992	114,261
Total..................	257,839,862	25,960,824

The inhabitants of the Slave States frequently
defend the institution of Slavery, on the ground that
it is necessary for the purposes of agriculture, asserting that their section of country represents the agricultural element of the Union, as the Free States
do the commercial. But if we examine the returns
of the seventh census of the United States (1850),
we shall discover that the North generally surpasses
the other section in produce common to both. With
regard to the staples of cotton, cane sugar, rice, and
tobacco, from the Slave States, we cannot do better
than give the following extract from Helper's *Crisis
of the South.* The figures are taken from official
returns.

"HAY CROP OF THE FREE STATES, 1850.

12,690,982 tons, at $11.20 = $142,138,998.

SUNDRY PRODUCTS OF THE SLAVE STATES, 1850.

Cotton	2,445,779 bales	at $32.00 =	$78,264,928
Tobacco ...	185,023,906 lbs.	„ .10 „	18,502,390
Rice (rough)	215,313,497 „	„ .04 „	8,612,539
Hay	1,137,784 tons	„ 11.20 „	12,743,180
Hemp	34,673 „	„ 112.00 „	3,883,376
Cane Sugar .	237,133,000 lbs.	„ .07 „	16,599,310

Total $138,605,723

Giving a balance of $3,533,275 in favour of the hay crop of the Free States against the entire value of the six staples of the South."

The same authority informs us that the proportion of landowners in the Slave States who are non-slaveholders is almost as 2 to 1, and he furnishes us with the following table:—

"LANDOWNERS IN THE SOUTHERN STATES.

Area of the South . . .	544,926,720 acres.	
Owned by Government. .	40,000,000 „	
„ Slaveholders .	173,024,000 „	
„ Non-slaveholders	331,902,720 „"	

VALUE OF LAND NORTH AND SOUTH.

Nothing will more clearly prove the damaging influence of Slavery than the small value of land in the Slave States. In 1850, the average value per acre, South, was $5.34, and in the South-west $6.26; whereas the Northern States averaged $28.07, and the North-western $11.39. A curious fact must not here be overlooked. In the elder Southern States land is of less value than in those of the South-west, newly settled; this is to be accounted for by the peculiar system of agriculture to which we have just referred.

This difference of value in the Free and Slave States is most marked and obvious on the courses of the rivers Missouri and Ohio, the land on one bank being several times more valuable than that opposite, traceable alone to the influence of the system prevailing in each State. The Slave-owners are compelled to admit that their plantations would become more valuable to them were they cultivated by free labour; but, in that case, the political pre-ponderance which Slavery has hitherto given them in the Confederation would no longer exist.

The Comptrollers of the States of New York and North Carolina give the following estimate of value of land in their respective States, in the year 1856:—

New York . . . . $36.97 per acre.
North Carolina . . . 3.06 „

When these two States commenced their career at the outset of the Republic, North Carolina numbered 53,631 inhabitants more than New York; her climate is better, and wood and water more plentiful; but, under the damaging influence of the Slave system, her land is now less than one-twelfth the value of that of the Free State, whilst her white population is only one-eighth.

RAILROADS.

The railroad system of a country is a pretty accurate test of its advancement, and we are enabled by the following returns to judge afresh the superiority of the North over the South. Railroads in the United States are constructed upon a widely different principle from those in Europe. A line is carried through territories not yet settled, munificent grants of the public lands being made to the company, who dispose of it in farms to emigrants, and thus defray the cost of construction. The invariable object is to push the works as rapidly as possible, the consequence being a defective permanent way, which eats up most of the eventual receipts in continued repairs. The following returns are not by any means perfect.

RAILROADS IN THE UNITED STATES AND RECEIPTS DURING TWELVE MONTHS.*

SLAVE STATES.

States.	Completed on January 1st, 1849.		Completed on January 1st, 1859.	
	Miles.	Dollars.	Miles.	Dollars.
Alabama	113	...	395	504,152
Arkansas	...	...	39	—
Delaware	17	146,291	93	95,413
Florida	54	...	119	—
Georgia	605	1,134,274	1,160	3,318,040
Kentucky	29	50,000	340	765,250
Louisiana	...	...	400	877,271
Maryland	360	1,468,829	639	4,957,403
Mississippi	117	...	657	1,933,733
Missouri	...	...	546	836,874
North Carolina......	254	...	763	1,086,005
South Carolina......	241½	800,073	733	3,239,729
Tennessee............	...	...	830	1,626,026
Texas	...	...	129	153,511
Virginia	371	...	1,230	2,925,806
District of Columbia	Included above.			
Total............	2,161½	3,599,467	8,073	22,319,213

* From the *American Almanac*, 1850, 1860.

FREE STATES.

States.	Completed on January 1st, 1849.		Completed on January 1st, 1859.	
	Miles.	Dollars.	Miles.	Dollars.
California............	...	...	22	—
Connecticut	229	432,803	594	2,415,503
Illinois	...	...	2,854	8,364,287
Indiana.........	86	468,529	1,284	2,869,850
Iowa	...	...	349	—
Maine	63	...	543	1,151,023
Massachusetts	1,058	5,910,667	1,457	8,211,322
Michigan	354½	427,430	1,073	3,382,219
New Hampshire	210	765,914	507	1,332,370
New Jersey	206¼	...	467	4,003,482
New York	840	3,951,904	2,580	18,572,552
Ohio.................	276	663,528	3,337	5,995,417
Pennsylvania........	973¾	121,350	2,317	11,138,295
Rhode Island........	50	182,572	65	208,439
Vermont	...	...	528	1,467,291
Wisconsin............	...	...	702	1,135,343
Minnesota............	250	graded in December, 1859.		
Total............	4,596½	12,924,697	18,679	70,247,393

BANKS.

The United States possess no national bank, it being one of the principles of the dominant Democratic party that such an institution should not be permitted to exist. The financial business of the country is carried on by means of private banks, the charters of which are in the hands of the authorities of the different States. The system obtaining in New York is that of the " free-banking law," and was introduced in 1838. By this law, any individual or association may engage in banking on depositing with the State Comptroller stocks of the United States or of any individual State (such stocks bearing 5 per cent. interest), or bonds and mortgages bearing at the rate of 6 per cent. per annum. On receipt of these securities, the parties applying are empowered to issue notes equal to the amount deposited. The Legislature revised this law in 1840. It is now required that the securities deposited shall consist of bonds and mortgages or stocks of the United States or New York State. By the same law, the banks of the city of New York are compelled to publish weekly returns of their transactions; and by a subsequent Act (Oct. 1853), a clearing-house was established in that city.

Similar laws have been passed in New Jersey, Illinois, Indiana, Wisconsin, Virginia, Tennessee, Lousiana, and Alabama. In the New England States, the banking laws are equally stringent, though upon a different system. No banks exist in California and Arkansas. The States not mentioned have banks chartered by special Acts of their various Legislatures.

BANKS, ETC., IN THE DIFFERENT STATES.

From their Returns nearest to January 1, 1859.

SLAVE STATES.

States.	Banks.	Capital.
		Dollars.
Alabama	6	3,663,490
Arkansas	None.	—
Delaware	12	1,638,185
Florida	—	No returns.
Georgia	28	12,479,111
Kentucky	37	12,216,725
Louisiana	12	24,215,689
Maryland	32	12,560,635
Mississippi.....................	2	1,110,600
Missouri	22	5,796,781
North Carolina	28	6,525,200
South Carolina	20	14,888,451
Tennessee	39	8,361,357
Texas	—	No returns.
Virginia......................	63	14,685,370
District of Columbia.........	—	No returns.
Total	301	118,141,594

FREE STATES.

States.	Banks.	Capital.
		Dollars.
California	None.	—
Connecticut	73	21,539,856
Illinois	48	4,000,334
Indiana	37	3,617,629
Iowa	—	No returns.
Maine	68	7,408,945
Massachusetts	174	61,819,825
Michigan	3	745,304
Minnesota	2	50,000
New Hampshire	52	5,041,000
New Jersey	46	7,359,122
New York....................	300	110,258,480
Ohio	53	6,707,151
Pennsylvania.................	87	24,565,805
Rhode Island.................	90	20,321,069
Vermont	41	4,082,416
Wisconsin	98	7,995,000
Oregon	—	No returns.
Total	1,172	285,511,936

IMPORTS AND CUSTOMS.

We have previously shown that the Southern States, from the year 1795 to 1816 inclusive, took the lead in Imports by about one million sterling over those of the North. Matters are considerably changed since then, for the report of the Secretary of the Federal Treasury, in relation to imports during the fiscal year terminating June 30th, 1858, proves that whilst the Free States entered goods to the value of $249,446,139, the entire South could only show $33,167,011. The great proportion of the latter came to New Orleans, the amount being nearly twenty millions of dollars, leaving thirteen millions to those ports which formerly surpassed the North in commercial activity. The Customs returns of 1854 amounted to $64,224,190, to which the South contributed $5,136,969. The United States' tariff has since been altered, and the returns in 1858 (to June 30th) were only $41,789,621 : if the above proportion be maintained, the South is not contributing very largely to the expenses of the general government, hich derives its receipts as follows :—

" STATEMENT OF THE UNITED STATES' REVENUE DURING THE
FISCAL YEAR ENDING JUNE 30TH, 1859.*

	Dollars.
Customs	49,565,824.38
Sale of public lands . .	1,756,687.30
Miscellaneous	2,082,559.33
Treasury notes . . .	9,667,400.00
Loan of 20,000,000 dols. .	18,620,000.00
Total yearly receipts .	81,692,471.01
Balance in Treasury .	6,398,316.10
Total	88,090,787.11 "

The money derived from the sale of public lands
must obviously come chiefly from emigrants, but it is
not directly so. When these lands are put into the
market, they are bought up by speculators at the rate
of $1.25 per acre (about 5s. 3d. English), and resold at
greatly advanced prices. This is a most iniquitous
system; but the speculators have always been too influential at Washington to allow of its being altered.
A Northern representative lately moved that the public
lands, when surveyed, should remain ten years before
being put up at public sale, in order to give immigrants the opportunity of settling thereon, and thus
avoid the fleecing operations of the speculators; but
the motion was defeated.

* *The American Almanack* for 1860.

The main source of revenue in the United States is the Customs duties; and the Southern States, at the present time, do not furnish more than from three to three and a half millions of dollars as their quota. Thus it has been for years; not merely with regard to one department of Government, but in all. If we examine the Postal statistics, we find the same rule obtaining—the Free States paying for the Slave.

POSTAL REVENUE.

By the official returns of the Post Office in 1855, we learn that the sum of $1,719,513 accrued from the sale of stamps in the Northern States, to $666,845 in the Southern. The three items of postage collected, registering of letters and newspapers realized $4,670,725 in the North, to $1,553,198 in the South; the total receipts from the Free States being $6,390,238 against $2,220,043 of the Slave. The cost of transmission of the mails was $2,608,295 in the former, to $2,385,953 in the latter. The returns of 1858 give the total cost of the Department at $7,198,816;—$3,402,865 for the North, and $3,795,951 for the South, to which the former contributed $5,335,560, and the latter only $1,810,355.

PRINCIPAL EMPLOYMENTS OF FREE MALE POPULA-
TION OVER FIFTEEN YEARS OF AGE, 1850.

SLAVE STATES.

States.	Commerce, Trade, Manufactures.	Agriculture.	Law, Medicine, Divinity.	Other Pursuits requiring Education.
Alabama	16,630	68,635	2,610	3,638
Arkansas	4,296	28,942	911	676
Delaware	5,633	7,884	251	581
Florida................	2,380	5,977	357	302
Georgia	20,715	83,362	2,815	3,942
Kentucky.............	36,598	115,017	3,811	4,420
Louisiana.............	32,879	18,639	1,827	2,444
Maryland.............	47,616	28,588	2,059	2,442
Mississippi	12,053	50,284	2,329	3,380
Missouri..............	30,098	65,561	2,893	3,147
North Carolina......	20,613	81,982	2,263	3,447
South Carolina......	13,205	41,302	1,829	3,161
Tennessee.............	23,432	118,979	3,363	3,589
Texas................	7,327	25,299	1,368	996
Virginia..............	52,675	108,364	4,791	5,622
District of Columbia	6,128	421	330	436
Total.............	332,278	849,236	33,807	42,223

PRINCIPAL EMPLOYMENTS, ETC.—*continued.*

FREE STATES.

States.	Commerce, Trade, Manufactures.	Agriculture.	Law, Medicine, Divinity.	Other Pursuits requiring Education.
California.........	69,007	2,059	876	198
Connecticut	38,653	31,881	1,614	2,162
Illinois	36,282	141,099	3,307	2,071
Indiana.............	45,318	163,229	4,229	3,031
Iowa...............	9,255	32,779	1,077	425
Maine	38,247	77,082	2,212	1,727
Massachusetts ...	146,002	55,699	4,702	5,371
Michigan	22,375	65,815	2,007	1,092
Minnesota*	656	563	68	37
New Hampshire.	27,905	47,440	1,642	1,425
New Jersey	46,544	32,834	1,731	2,457
New York.........	312,697	313,980	14,258	11,104
Ohio...............	142,687	270,362	9,001	8,263
Pennsylvania	266,927	207,495	9,954	10,830
Rhode Island	21,004	8,482	556	881
Vermont	17,063	48,327	1,827	1,563
Wisconsin	20,526	40,980	1,477	800
Total.........	1,261,098	1,542,106	60,648	53,437

* Then only a territory.

EDUCATION AND INTELLIGENCE.

In comparing the Free and Slave States, with reference to their educational facilities and intellectual advancement, the vast superiority of the former is strikingly apparent. To use an expression frequently heard in the northern portion of the Union, "the South only produces niggers and cotton." Schools certainly exist there, but the instruction afforded is of the most meagre description, and the colleges are so mediocre, that the well-to-do Southern community send their children to the North to be educated. Grievous are the complaints made by Southern statesmen in consequence; for the young men return home with consciences unsettled as to the sound policy and the justice of Slave-holding. The school-books used throughout the Union are nearly all of Free State origin, and the alternative is presented of no education or education antagonistic to the " peculiar institution." One of the leading journals of Virginia has lately bemoaned this fact in the following words :—

" It is the insinuations, nay, assertions of the moral wrong of Slavery which our youths read in these Northern school-books, which give an early bias to their impressions—impressions upon which they do not reason; and

4

the result is, that when they come to their second childhood, in their last wills and testaments, they liberate their Slaves, and fill the country with a miserable herd of free negroes."
—*Richmond Enquirer.*

The men of literature, science, and the arts belong to ·the North. Bancroft, Prescott, Irving, Bryant, Halleck, Whittier, Longfellow, Willis, Cooper, are all Northern men, and Story and Kent, amongst law-writers, belong to the same section.

The *Crisis of the South* furnishes us with the following statement as to the proportion of white adults over twenty years of age who cannot read and write. The figures are given on the authority of the census returns of the United States :—

" FREE STATES.		SLAVE STATES.	
Connecticut . . 1 in 568		Louisiana` . . . 1 in 38½	
Vermont . . . „ 473		Maryland . . . „ 27	
New Hampshire . „ 310		Mississippi . . . „ 20	
Massachusetts . „ 166		Delaware . . . „ 18	
Maine . . . . „ 108		South Carolina . „ 17	
Michigan . . . „ 97		Missouri . . . „ 16	
Rhode Island . . „ 67		Alabama . . . „ 15	
New Jersey . . „ 58		Kentucky . . . „ 13½	
New York . . „ 56		Georgia . . . . „ 13	
Pennsylvania . „ 50		Virginia . . . „ 12½	
Ohio . . . . „ 43		Arkansas . . . „ 11½	
Indiana . . . „ 18		Tennessee . . . „ 11	
Illinois . . . „ 17		North Carolina . „ 7 "	

In comparing these two results, it must be remembered that Southern ignorance is *native*, the Northern, *imported*. The vast stream of European emigration avoids the Slave districts, seeking the free prairie lands of the west. Ohio, and more especially Indiana and Illinois, receive the major portion of the emigrants, and this accounts for their proportion being so much lower than the other northern States.

The educational returns for 1858-59 are not quite complete. We find by the *American Almanac*, that there are now existing in the Free States upwards of 87,000 public schools, involving an annual expense of 16,545,288 dols. In the South, the schools do not reach 15,000 in number, and the yearly amount expended upon them is less than two and a quarter millions of dollars.

SCHOLASTIC INSTITUTIONS IN THE UNITED STATES, 1850.

SLAVE STATES.

States.	Number of Public Schools.	Pupils.	Academies.	Colleges.
Alabama	1,152	28,380	166	5
Arkansas	353	8,493	90	3
Delaware	194	8,970	65	2
Florida	69	1,878	34	—
Georgia	1,251	32,705	219	13
Kentucky	2,234	71,429	330	15
Louisiana	664	25,046	143	5
Maryland	907	33,254	224	11
Mississippi	782	18,746	171	11
Missouri	1,570	51,754	204	9
North Carolina......	2,657	104,095	272	5
South Carolina......	724	17,838	202	8
Tennessee.....	2,667	103,651	260	17
Texas	349	7,946	97	2
Virginia	2,937	67,438	303	12
District of Columbia	22	2,169	47	2
Total.........	18,532	583,792	2,827	120

FREE STATES.

States.	Number of Public Schools.	Pupils.	Academies.	Colleges.
California............	2	49	6	—
Connecticut	1,656	71,269	202	4
Illinois	4,054	125,790	81	6
Indiana	4,822	161,500	130	11
Iowa..................	742	29,616	31	2
Maine	4,042	192,815	131	3
Massachusetts	3,679	176,475	381	6
Michigan	2,714	110,455	37	3
New Hampshire ...	2,381	75,643	107	1
New Jersey	1,479	78,205	219	4
New York	11,580	675,221	883	18
Ohio..................	11,661	484,153	206	26
Pennsylvania	9,061	413,706	524	21
Rhode Island	416	23,130	46	1
Vermont	2,731	93,457	118	5
Wisconsin	1,423	58,817	58	2
Minnesota*	...	...	1	—
Total.........	62,443	2,770,301	3,172	113

* Then only a territory.

PUBLIC LIBRARIES, ETC. IN THE UNITED STATES, 1850.

SLAVE STATES.

States.	No. of Libra- ries.*	No. of Volumes.*	Authors	Pub- lishers.	Book- sellers.
Alabama	37	18,077	1	...	4
Arkansas	1	1,000	—	—	—
Delaware	5	16,700	...	...	2
Florida	4	5,537	...	...	3
Georgia	24	35,632	1	1	11
Kentucky	27	63,440	2	3	43
Louisiana	6	30,000	...	2	27
Maryland	46	84,565	...	10	67
Mississippi	108	15,650	...	2	6
Missouri	19	37,506	...	...	29
North Carolina	8	24,247	1	...	9
South Carolina	14	59,914	...	1	16
Tennessee	21	47,356	1	1	9
Texas	4	1,631	...	4	3
Virginia	30	89,180	...	...	35
Dist. of Columbia	20	148,673	3	...	19
Total	374	679,108	9	24	283

* Compiled by the Smithsonian Institute, Washington.

FREE STATES.

States.	No. of Libraries.*	No. of Volumes.*	Authors	Publishers.	Booksellers.
California	...	...	...	1	3
Connecticut	19	98,638	4	10	35
Illinois	27	19,916	...	12	21
Indiana	16	40,000	1	4	21
Iowa	5	2,660	...	...	2
Maine	31	56,856	...	7	32
Massachusetts ...	762	415,658	17	51	189
Michigan	381	65,235	2	5	7
Minnesota	2	3,200	—	—	—
New Hampshire.	50	57,178	...	...	24
New Jersey	17	46,305	3	7	35
New York.........	8,284	1,756,254	28	133	456
Ohio	48	104,634	4	23	157
Pennsylvania	80	287,519	13	72	402
Rhode Island......	45	79,341	...	...	21
Vermont	23	34,299	1	...	18
Wisconsin.........	35	7,163	...	6	14
Total.........	9,825	3,074,856	73	331	1,437

* Compiled by the Smithsonian Institute, Washington.

PERIODICALS IN THE UNITED STATES IN 1850.

SLAVE STATES.

States.	Daily.	Semi and Tri Weekly.	Weekly.	Semi-Monthly.	Monthly and Quarterly.
Alabama	6	5	48	1	—
Arkansas	...	...	9	—	—
Delaware	...	3	7	—	—
Florida.............	...	1	9	—	—
Georgia	5	3	37	6	—
Kentucky.........	9	7	38	8	—
Louisiana	11	6	37	...	1
Maryland	6	4	54	1	3
Mississippi	...	4	46	—	—
Missouri	5	4	45	...	7
North Carolina ..	...	5	40	6	—
South Carolina...	7	5	27	5	2
Tennessee.........	8	2	36	...	4
Texas	...	5	29	—	—
Virginia...........	15	12	55	3	2
Dist. of Columbia	5	5	8	—	—
Total.........	77	71	525	30	19

FREE STATES.

States.	Daily.	Semi and Tri Weekly.	Weekly.	Semi-Monthly.	Monthly and Quarterly.
California.........	4	...	3	—	—
Connecticut	7	4	30	...	3
Illinois	8	4	84	3	8
Indiana............	9	2	95	1	...
Iowa...............	...	2	25	...	2
Maine	4	5	39	...	1
Massachusetts ...	22	15	126	3	36
Michigan	3	2	47	3	3
Minnesota	—	—	—	—	—
New Hampshire..	...	...	35	1	2
New Jersey	6	...	43	2	—
New York........	51	21	308	9	39
Ohio..............	26	10	201	23	1
Pennsylvania.....	24	3	261	19	2
Rhode Island.....	5	2	12	—	—
Vermont..........	2	1	30	...	2
Wisconsin........	6	4	35	...	1
Total.........	177	75	1,374	64	100

But the aggregate circulation of the Northern press, as compared with that of the Southern States, still further evinces the superiority of the former. The following table gives the circulation of the various periodicals in the Slave districts during the year 1849–50, on authority of the United States Census Commissioners :—

Alabama	2,662,741
Arkansas	377,000
Delaware	421,200
Florida	319,800
Georgia	4,070,866
Kentucky	6,582,838
Louisiana	12,416,224
Maryland	19,612,724
Mississippi	1,752,504
Missouri	6,195,560
North Carolina	2,020,564
South Carolina	7,145,930
Tennessee	6,940,750
Texas	1,296,924
Virginia	9,223,068
District of Columbia	11,127,236
Total circulation	92,165,929

The gross circulation of the Northern press during the same year was 334,244,049; the single State of

New York exceeding the entire South by upwards of 23 millions of copies.

REASONS WHY THE SOUTH HAS HITHERTO DOMINATED THE UNION.

After an examination of these various returns, the inquiry will naturally present itself—" How is it possible that the North, so much and so long the superior of the South in wealth, civilization, and numbers, can have allowed itself thus to be dominated by the minority?" The answer lies in the fact, that whilst the Northern States have been engaged in the different branches of commerce, the South has had but one object in view—the preservation and extension of its peculiar institution.

Until lately, only two political parties existed in the Union—the Federalists, or Whigs, whose aim was centralization; and the Democratic, or States' rights party, who maintained that power was derived from the States alone.   To all intents and purposes, the Whigs represented the conservative element, the Democrats the liberal.   But, in process of time, new issues presented themselves.   The Northern States became over-crowded; whilst the land in the South became exhausted, by the peculiarity of its cultivation. Emigration was the only alternative for the people of both sections, and the unoccupied territories of the Confederation offered themselves alike to Free and Slave labour. The fathers of the Republic, at an early period, recognized the fact that the two systems could not long exist together, and from the first Congress of the Union until Mr. Fillmore's elevation to the presidency, the policy of the country was in favour of the curtailment of Slavery.

The Slave-trade was denounced by Congress as early as 1774, the colonies being pledged to disclaim any connection whatever with it. Ten years subsequently, within three months of the evacuation of the British army, the leaders of the revolution sought to rid their new-born country of a blight fixed upon them, not of their own seeking, but entirely against their wishes. It was not, however, possible to rid the Southern States of their Slaves by a simple ordinance, or to forthwith substitute free for forced labour. But it was perfectly feasible to prevent the future growth of Slavery, by forbidding its extension into new territory; and this the far-seeing statesmen of the Republic hastened to effect.

One of the final acts of the Continental Congress was the passing, in 1787, of the Ordinance for the governing of the North-west Territory. This territory consisted of land beyond the Ohio, ceded by the different States to the Federal Government, free of all conditions whatever. It was resolved by the Congress, in behalf of the whole Confederation, that involuntary servitude, except for crime, should for ever be excluded from this territory. We shall, hereafter, see how the South evaded this Ordinance.

On the 1st of March, 1784, Thomas Jefferson had brought into Congress the report of the Committee on Territories, a majority of this committee being representatives of Southern States. This report, which is known as the "Jeffersonian Ordinance of 1784," declared as follows :—

" *Resolved,*—That the territory ceded, or to be ceded, by individual States to the United States, whensoever the same shall have been purchased of the Indian inhabitants and offered for sale by the United States, shall be formed into additional States, bounded in the following manner " (states the boundary lines). Then follow resolutions as to settlers in the territory forming temporary governments, previous to their admission into the Union as States, and the mode of such admission, concluding with the following proviso:—" *Provided, that both the temporary and permanent governments be established on these principles as their basis :—*

" 1. That they shall for ever remain a part of the United States of America.

" 2. That in their persons, property, and territory, they

shall be subject to the Government of the United States in
Congress assembled, and to the Articles of Confederation
in all those cases in which the original States shall be so
subject.

" 3. That they shall be subject to pay a part of the
Federal debts, contracted or to be contracted, to be ap-
propriated on them by Congress, according to the same
common rule and measure by which apportionments thereof
shall be made on the other States.

" 4. That their respective governments shall be in republican forms, and shall admit no person to be a citizen
who holds any hereditary title.

" 5. *That after the year* 1800 *of the Christian era, there
shall be neither Slavery nor involuntary servitude in any of
the said States,* otherwise than in punishment of crimes,
whereof the party shall have been duly convicted to have
been personally guilty," &c. &c.

This latter clause was finally lost, the majority not
being sufficient to carry it into law; but its very
proposal by Mr. Jefferson, the father of the constitution of the United States, and the citizen of a Slave
State, proves what ideas were held upon this subject
by the founders of the Republic.

Washington, born and bred amongst the Slave-
holding hierarchy, recognized the injustice and im-
policy of the system, and stamped the seal of his
disapprobation upon it by finally freeing all his Slaves.
In his speeches and correspondence, he frequently

expressed his earnest desire that some general plan might be introduced for the manumission of all negroes throughout the different States; nor was he alone in this desire. Adams, Madison, Franklin, Jay—in fact, all the leading men of the new-born Republic—loudly and continually endorsed the opinion of Milton, that "no man who knows aught can be so stupid as to deny that all men naturally were born free, being the image and semblance of God himself, and were, by privilege, above all the creatures, born to command and not to obey."

Nowhere in the Constitution of the United States is Slavery recognized, or even referred to. The framers of that Constitution studiously avoided any reference to it; lest they might be considered to have in some manner endorsed it. So guarded were they, that when discussing the question of a tariff, they at first declined to raise any revenue from the importation of negroes, lest their so doing might be construed into the recognition of negroes as property. Mr. Madison, subsequently President of the Republic, stated his firm conviction that "it would be wrong to admit there could be property in man."

Nor was the idea of the total injustice of Slavery maintained by statesmen alone. The Supreme Courts of Mississippi and Kentucky, viewing it in a strictly legal point of view, subsequently characterized it as follows. The former declared,—" Slavery is condemned by reason and the laws of nature. It exists, and can only exist, through municipal regulations."

The Kentucky jurists coincided with the above opinion, in these words :—" We view this as a right existing by positive law of a municipal character, without foundation in the law of nature, or the written and common law."

These good men and true patriots were, however, unable to carry their benevolent designs into effect, the self-interest of the planters presenting an insurmountable obstacle. The three Slave States of North and South Carolina and Georgia paralyzed their efforts, and even, for the moment, prevented their putting a stop to the Slave-trade. When the subject of immediate relinquishment was discussed, the representatives of those States openly declared that they would never consent to such a measure, and it was postponed some years in consequence. They were, however, mainly assisted by the dastard conduct of the Northern States, who gave up their advocacy of immediate abolition of the trade, in consideration of the South not opposing their Navigation Acts. Bitterly have the Free States paid for this their first iniquitous compromise.

But though the Federal Government failed in immediately abolishing the Slave-trade, it succeeded in preventing the carrying of Slaves into the Western territory, and, finally, in the year 1800, Congress passed an Act forbidding the further carrying on of the trade, the penalties being forfeiture of the vessel, and a fine of $1,000 for every negro imported.

The Slaveholders were, however, too powerful an interest to resign the struggle, and the attempt was made in 1803 to revise these Acts of the General Government. The immense territory then known as Indiana, and which now includes the State of that name, and also Illinois, Michigan, and Wisconsin, petitioned Congress to revoke its ordinance of 1787, and to grant them permission to employ Slave labour, on the ground that immigration was totally insufficient to develop the resources of the country. In answer to this request, the Committee on Territories, by its chairman, Mr. Randolph, reported that it was "highly dangerous and inexpedient to impair a provision wisely instituted to promote the happiness and prosperity of the North-Western country, and to give strength and security to that extensive frontier." And when the attempt was again made during the following year, and three years subsequently, to introduce Slavery into the territory, Congress stood stedfastly upon its first decision.

Although opposed to any further extension of Slavery, Congress was forced to submit to the legalization of it in Kentucky, when that State applied for admission into the Union, under the threat of Kentucky's uniting herself to Spain. This was again the case with the territories ceded to the Confederation by Georgia and North Carolina, such cession being made with the proviso that Slavery should be permitted therein: the territory so ceded has since become the Slave States of Tennessee, Mississippi, and Alabama. In later years we have seen similar demands made by Texas, which entered the Union with the understanding that she should hereafter be divided into five States, Slavery existing in all.

The determination of South Carolina to reopen, if possible, the Slave-trade, brought about the enactment of the laws of 1808, 1818, 1819, and 1820, the last declaring the traffic to be piracy, and punishable with death.

We have now arrived at the period when the Slaveholding oligarchy began to feel themselves sufficiently powerful to brave the indignation of the Nortaern States, and to initiate that villanous policy which has dominated the Union for the past forty years.

THE MISSOURI COMPROMISE.

The legislation of Congress had, until this period, been generally in favour of freedom. Louisiana had been admitted into the Union as a Slave State, but, like Kentucky, the case was exceptional; for when purchased from the French Government, Slavery had existed there, by law, for years. The Louisianian territory not included within that portion which had entered the Union as a State, covered an immense area, embracing what are now the States of Arkansas and Missouri, and the Nebraska-Kansas territory. Arkansas and Missouri had become sufficiently peopled to apply for admission into the Confederation, and it lay within the province of Congress to declare whether they should enter the Union with or without Slavery. The question of free or forced labour now presented itself, and divided the country into two camps. The House of Representatives ranged itself on the side of freedom, whilst the upper House, or Senate, maintained that Slavery was legal in all the Louisianian territory. For three long years the struggle lasted, the House of Representatives refusing to admit Missouri with " the peculiar institution,"

and the Senate persisting in returning the bill for
reconsideration. The Southern States, finding the
North resolutely opposed their nefarious designs, and
that their object could not be obtained by intimida-
tion or threats of disunion, threw a sop to the Free
States in what is known as the " Missouri Compromise." In consideration of the territory comprised
within the State of Missouri being admitted into the
Union as a Slave State, it was declared that henceforward and for evermore human bondage, except
for crimes committed, should not pass the line
36° 30′ of north latitude.

No act of the American Congress has been of so
solemn a character as this memorable Compromise.
It was the reconciliation of a people—the oath of an
entire nation. For three long years the struggle
had continued, until civil war loomed in the near
future. Statesmen despaired of their country, whilst
the South persisted, and the North sullenly refused
its consent. But this olive-branch of peace calmed
the contending parties, and the Free States agreed to
the admission of Missouri, relying implicitly upon
the oath of the South, that Slavery should not, henceforth, be permitted north or west of the new State.

" Man proposes, but God disposes." Infinite truth
has vetoed all such unhallowed compromises, and

placed an irreconcilable antagonism between Slavery and Freedom. In His almighty wisdom the sin carries with it its own punishment, and the *penalty* is the resulting necessity of the *crime.* The North had consented to the enslavement of Missouri, in order that Kansas and the other territories might be free. Kansas is invaded *by Missourians;* her towns besieged, her people murdered, and her liberties enslaved.

The Southern States, having introduced the thin end of the wedge, slowly prepared for the struggle which they well knew must inevitably ensue. Having gained the victory on the first trial of strength, they turned their attention to the organization of parties, in readiness for the moment when their policy should be that of Danton, " *De l' audace, encore de l' audace, et toujours de l' audace.*"

From the moment of the admission of Missouri into the Union, there were, practically, but two parties in the country—Slavery extensionists and Slavery prohibitionists. Old party names were retained, but adapted to the situation, and we now heard of " National Whigs " and " National Democrats," the signification being, that however much they might differ as Whigs and Democrats, *they were in unison upon the question of fostering the " peculiar institution.*" The population of the Free States increased more rapidly than in other portions of the Union; and unless they could put into operation the old maxim, " *diviser pour régner,*" the advantage already gained might slip from their grasp.

With Belial-like cunning, the South succeeded in turning the very element of Northern strength to its own advantage. The countless hordes of European emigrants were to be acted upon, influenced, seduced. These Irishmen and Germans, uneducated serfs of the old world, avoided the area of Slave labour, settling upon the fruitful plains of the far-spreading West. By means of its emissaries and managing committees in the Northern ports, Southern politicians induced these immigrants to remain in the districts of great cities, such as New York, Philadelphia, and other populous localities, wherever, in fact, their votes could be made to tell upon the State elections. The Catholic priesthood, ready as it ever was—ready as the clergy of every religion, sect, and age—to sacri-fice political liberty to the aggrandisement of their church, were flattered and gained over. The count-less petty offices of town and county were given up to foreign nominees. The police force of Northern cities became almost entirely Irish, who also, with a sprinkling of Germans, divided the duties and emoluments of aldermen, common councilmen, coroners, magistrates, &c., and, in return, gave the assistance of their votes and passions to the National Democratic party. The latter gained doubly by the arrangement. They gained not merely "the foreign vote," but that opposing interest which could not be bought over—the educated masses of the Northern cities —who eventually were driven from the polls and sickened of politics, by seeing into what hands public affairs had fallen. This was, in after years, the cause of the rise of the Know-Nothing or American party.

Having thus secured a constantly increasing body of adherents, the South was not long in proving to Northern politicians that the surest road to self-advancement was "in keeping step to the music of the Union"—another *national* expression, signifying the union of Slavery with the acts of the General Government. Northern politicians were not slow in appreciating the situation. They remarked, as they could not help remarking, that the Southern States were one at the polls, and that they possessed efficient supporters in the North. They, therefore, courted this influence, and openly gloried in being "Northern men with Southern principles."

One of the greatest and best men of the United States, one of the greatest and best of any country—

Henry Clay—was defeated in his contest for the Presidency by this organized band of Northern traitors and slave-like foreigners. True he was a Southerner, but, if we may be allowed the expression, "a Southern man with Northern principles," being stedfastly opposed to any further spread of Slavery. Daniel Webster, the Expounder of the Constitution and the first statesman of his country, never had a chance of the Presidency, owing to his labours in the cause of freedom. The South gives not its influence to such men as these, but to politicians of the calibre of Mr. Franklin Pierce or the "facile" Mr. Buchanan, having previously assured itself that not the slightest taint of free-soil proclivity can be discovered in their antecedents.

The observation has been made that "*the South never performed its dirty work by Southern hands.*" The triumphs of the Slave power have been achieved under Northern presidents, elected and governed by the Southern oligarchy; whilst Slavery has invariably been checked when a Southerner occupied the White House. It is during the administrations of the last three chief magistrates of the Republic that Slavery has dominated the councils of the nation, tyrannizing the free white men of the North, and initiating the present reign of terror and proscription.

THE FUGITIVE SLAVE ACT.

The Slave oligarchy, having forged the weapon, now prepared to use it. Their first object was to commit the Federal Government to their aims, and this they effected by means of the Fugitive Slave Act of 1850,—a measure of remorseless tyranny which can scarcely find a parallel in the history of any other country. Hitherto the Federal enactments had been more or less favourable to liberty, and, as much as possible, non-committal upon the question of property in the Slave; but this Act constituted the " chattel " not merely " property," but more emphatically property than anything else a man could possess. Run away with a citizen's watch, purse, cattle, wife, or child, his only remedy was in the *State* tribunals; but assist his black servant to escape, and the whole power of the *Confederation* aided him in the recapture. All the safeguards of justice were revoked by this measure. The poor coloured man—it mattered little whether slave or not, whether just escaped from bondage, or the resident of many years in a Free State—became liable, at any moment, to be seized and carried south. Any man calling himself the citizen of a Slave State could enter the United States District Court of his State, and declare, *on affidavit simply*, that such and such an one was his " property " and a fugitive from labour, and every Federal officer throughout the Union forthwith became a bloodhound to hunt out the fugitive and restore him to his owner.   The affidavit was forwarded to the United States court of the district where the poor outcast had taken refuge; he was seized and carried to the nearest jail, the Habeas Corpus Act suspended, and trial by jury denied him.   The Act directed that the proceedings should be summary, before a petty magistrate appointed by the Court and holding office during its will and pleasure; that this magistrate should receive remuneration, not from a salary, but from fees, *in proportion to the number of unfortunates he sent back to Slavery;* that evidence should be *ex parte*, and that the offender should not be heard in his own defence, or by counsel.

The advocates of the Fugitive Slave Act knew they were attacking the conscience of the North, and that their measure would meet with almost universal opposition, and they therefore embodied the following penalties in the bill:—All marshals and deputy-marshals of the United States—that is to say, *Federal officers*—were bound to assist in the capture, under penalty of a fine of 200*l.* and the full value of the slave if he escaped them.   They were empowered to call upon bystanders to render assistance, and could summon the *posse comitatus;* whilst all and every expense attending upon the capture and final rendition was to be ;defrayed out of the treasury of the Confederation. Obstructors, concealers of fugitives, or any assisting in their escape, were condemned in a penalty of 200*l.* to the General Government, a like amount to the supposed owner, and imprisonment for six months. The Northern States, by their senators and representatives, opposed the passing of the measure without success. The South triumphed, and prepared for still further demands.

But why should we speak in the past tense, as though the Fugitive Slave Act were a thing of history, a dead letter upon the statutes? This glorious product of slaveholding liberty, this trophy of Southern legislation, this emanation of hell, is the still enforced, the living law of the United States.

THE FOREIGN POLICY OF THE PRO-SLAVERY PARTY.
—ANNEXATION AND FILIBUSTERISM.

Careful not to offend the North too rapidly, the Slave oligarchy now turned its attention outside the Union, and commenced filibustering attempts southward. Central America, Cuba, and Mexico, suffered continual raids from armed bands, composed almost exclusively of Southern men, and officered and equipped by them. The Government at Washington *publicly* disowned these attempts, knowing at the same time that the Legislatures of various Southern States were finding equipments for the robbers from their arsenals, and funds from their treasuries. The object of the South—for most of the leaders of that section of the country were interested in the plot—was preponderance at Washington. If they could annex any one of the above-mentioned countries, they would immediately add three or four additional States to the Confederation, representing twice the number of United States Senators, and a proportionate number of Representatives in the Lower House. But the North saw through their object, and if Cuba, Costa Rica, or Mexico do not now belong to the Union, *it is only because the Free States would not consent to the annexation. At any time during these ten years, one or all of those countries could have been Americanized, in defiance of any Government in Europe.* The people of the United States number upwards of 30,000,000; the whole population is accustomed to the use of arms from their youth up; their resources are infinite; their public debt next to nothing; and they are within a stone's throw of their object. Nothing else prevented the consummation but the determination of the Northern States to oppose the policy of the South; and we shall find, on examination, that the leaders of public opinion in the Free States have always been the firmest opponents of filibusterism and annexation.

That the extension of Slavery is the sole cause of this brigand policy was pointedly asserted by Senator Seward no later than March last. Mr. Seward says:—

" Citizens of the United States, in the spirit of this policy, subverted the free Republic of Nicaragua, and opened it to Slavery and the African Slave-trade, and held it in that condition, waiting annexation to the United States, until its sovereignty was restored by a combination of sister republics exposed to the same danger, and apprehensive of similar subversion.

" For this policy, so far as the Government has sanctioned it, the Democratic party avows itself responsible. Everywhere complaint against it is denounced, and its opponents proscribed. Official integrity has been cause for rebuke and punishment, when it resisted frauds designed to promote the extension of Slavery. Throughout the whole Republic there is not one known dissenter from that policy remaining in place, if within reach of the executive arm. Nor over the face of the whole world is there to be found a representative of our country who is not an apologist for the extension of Slavery.

" It is in America that these things have happened. In
the nineteenth century, the era of the world's greatest
progress, and while all nations but ourselves have been
either abridging or altogether suppressing commerce in
men; at the very moment when the Russian serf is emancipated, and the Georgian captive, the Nubian prisoner,
and the Abyssinian savage are lifted up to freedom by the
successor of Mohammed. The world, prepossessed in our
behalf by our early devotion to the rights of human
nature, as no nation ever before engaged its respect and
sympathies, asks, in wonder and amazement, what all this
demoralization means."

It is but right that Englishmen should know who
are the causes of these vile attempts periodically
made upon the independence of neighbouring States.
They all proceed from that party whose one great
aim is the perpetuation and extension of Slavery. It
was the advocacy, the championship of this policy
which caused Mr. Buchanan to be the nominee of
the dominant party in the Union at the last Presidential election, and he has directed the concerns
of his country during the past four years, because
he stood pledged to the Slave oligarchy to do his
utmost to annex Cuba to the Confederation.

During the administration of General Pierce, the
pro-Slavery democracy determined upon making a
violent effort to obtain the island of Cuba, and Mr.

Soulé, United States plenipotentiary to the Court of Madrid, was charged with the mission of effecting a purchase. Mr. Soulé, an emigrant Frenchman, naturalized in the State of Louisiana, had obtained this advancement to the dignity of ambassador on account of his ultra pro-Slavery and democratic principles. Since his relinquishment of diplomatic functions he has devoted himself to the development of filibusterism, being the recognized agent and factotum of the celebrated William Walker, of Nicaragua infamy. No more suitable envoy could be selected for forcing a sale of Cuba at the buyer's own price; but the democratic party in the Southern States well knew that the mission would be one of difficulty, and orders were, therefore, sent out by the President to the American Ministers at the Courts of St. James (Mr. Buchanan) and the Tuileries (Mr. Mason) to meet Mr. Soulé and confer with him as to the speediest mode of obtaining the desired result. The Ministers to England and France were selected, not merely on account of their offices being the most important in the American diplomatic corps, but because the governments of those two countries were understood to be the protectors of Spain and the guaranteers of her possessions in the Antilles. The three plenipotentiaries met, first at Ostend, and subsequently at Aix-la-Chapelle. The result of their deliberations was the paper known in the United States as the " Ostend Manifesto," from which we make the following *verbatim* quotations. We trust our readers will peruse these different paragraphs with attention, for the Ostend Manifesto is not merely important as the expression of opinion of three prominent statesmen, but it is also " the destiny," the rule of action in foreign affairs of the pro-Slavery American Democracy.

" We have arrived at the conclusion, and are thoroughly convinced, that an immediate and earnest effort ought to be made by the Government of the United States to purchase Cuba from Spain at any price for which it can be obtained, not exceeding the sum of   dollars.
. . . .

" We firmly believe, that in the progress of human events, the time has arrived when the vital interests of Spain are as seriously involved in the sale, as those of the United States in the purchase of the island ; and that the transaction will prove equally honourable to both nations. Under these circumstances, we cannot anticipate a failure, unless possibly through the malign influence of foreign powers, who possess no right whatever to interfere in the matter. . . . .

" It must be clear to every reflecting mind, that from the peculiarity of its geographical position, and the considerations attendant on it, Cuba is as necessary to the

North American Republic, as any of its present members, and that it belongs naturally to that great family of States, of which the Union is the providential nursery. . . . .

. " Indeed, the Union can never enjoy repose, nor possess reliable security, as long as Cuba is not embraced within its boundaries. . . . .

" Considerations exist which render delay in the acquisition of this island exceedingly dangerous to the United States. . . . .

" Cuba has thus become to us an unceasing danger, and a permanent cause of anxiety and alarm."

(This extraordinary diplomatic paper having offered a price for the island, and informed the Spanish people that they must have it by fair means, if possible, fixes its own value on the proposed purchase, tells Spain she is in want of the money, and coolly suggests how she should use that money when she has got it. Thus: " Two-thirds of this sum, if employed in the construction of a system of railroads," &c. &c. " This object once accomplished, Spain would become a centre of attraction for the travelling world.")

The Manifesto continues :—

" But Spain is in imminent danger of losing Cuba without remuneration. Extreme oppression, it is now universally admitted, justifies any people in endeavouring to relieve themselves from the yoke of their oppressors.

6

. . . . We know that the President is justly inflexible
in his determination to execute the neutrality laws; but
should the Cubans themselves rise in revolt against the
oppression which they suffer, no human power could
prevent citizens of the United States, and liberal-minded
men of other countries, from rushing to their assistance.
. . . . It is not improbable, therefore, that Cuba
may be wrested from Spain by a successful revolution;
and, in that event, she will not only lose the island, but the
price which we are now willing to pay for it. . . . .

" But if Spain, deaf to the voice of her own interest,
and actuated by stubborn pride and a false sense of honour,
should refuse to sell Cuba to the United States, then the
question will arise—what ought to be the course of the
American Government under such circumstances? . . . .

" After we shall have offered Spain a price for Cuba
far beyond its present value, and this shall have been
refused, it will then be time to consider the question—does
Cuba, in the possession of Spain, seriously endanger our
internal peace and the existence of our cherished Union?
Should this question be answered in the affirmative, then
by every law, human and divine, we shall be justified in
wresting it from Spain, if we possess the power."

Is there in the whole range of diplomacy so vile a
document as this? The only excuse which any of
the pro-Slavery band can give for it is the specious
one that the Manifesto was not intended for aught
else than the guidance of the President of the United
States. But it is precisely because the principles it

advocates, and the line of action it suggests, were intended for home consumption, that it is so monstrous. As the private or *sub rosâ* opinion of three men, even though ambassadors, it might pass ; for it would not necessarily be indorsed by their Government. As their recommendation to the Washington Cabinet of a certain policy, *such recommendation being suggested previously to them in their instructions,* the document might again be overlooked; for the Cabinet did not necessarily represent public opinion in the Union, and no action could be taken upon foreign questions without consent of Congress.   Not for these two reasons was the Ostend Manifesto so fraught with danger to the peace of the world.   It was, and *it is* because Messrs. Buchanan, Mason, Soulé, and Pierce, acting for the Democratic party, desired to show to England, France, and Spain, that, sooner or later, Cuba must, *should,* belong to the United States ; and in order that they might hereafter be able to say to Spain, in justification of their seizing it,—*" Why didn't you take our dollars when we offered them ? We told you how it would be."*

There remained a hidden meaning in the document which only the initiated might understand.—" Should the Cubans themselves rise in revolt against the oppression which they suffer, no human power could

prevent citizens of the United States from rushing to
their assistance." It is now well known throughout
the Confederation, that a regularly organized body
exists in the Southern States, which is gradually
" Americanizing " the island, enlisting the disaffected
Cubans in a secret society, and preparing them for
the signal to rise—a signal which will come from
American Slaveholders when they know the forces of
the Confederation are ready to back them. This
band of conspirators, whose rallying point is New
Orleans, has existed for several years, their proceedings being winked at by successive Administrations, until the Ostend Manifesto gave them a *quasi*
endorsement, and Buchanan and Co. told them,—"*Get
the crop ready and we'll help you to cut it.*"

Why will not Englishmen think it worth their while
to seek out causes in this entanglement of filibustering
effects? Here have we been crying out for years
against the annexationist policy of the American
Government, paying millions for the support of fleets
in the West Indies to maintain our influence, and on
the Coast of Africa, to prevent the Slave-trade; all
the while condemning, *in spite of evidence to the contrary,* a whole people for the crime of a few. There
are not 400,000 Slaveholders in the United States.
The millions, South and North, who hate Slavery

as we do, are not responsible for these outrages on the law of nations, on the peace of the world. The Free States have, till lately, devoted their attention solely to commerce, and commerce flourishes only in peace and amity with other nations. Roused by the atrocities committed upon themselves by this same Slave power, roused by the disgrace brought upon their common country by the freebooters of the South, they are now stretching forth their hands to grasp the reins of Government. Read the works and speeches of Northern Free-State politicians on this annexationist policy of their antagonists. By no European statesman whatever is it more strongly and continuously condemned, than by the Sewards, Chases, Greeleys, and other leaders of the Republican majority. Shall we not watch their struggle with interest, and wish them God speed on their mission of "peace and good-will toward men?"

Lest it might be thought that this Ostend Manifesto is but the proposal of a diplomatic clique, we shall now give the endorsement of the Democratic party, copied *verbatim* from the declaration of their principles at the Cincinnati Convention of 1856.

" 1. *Resolved,*—That there are questions connected with the foreign policy of this country which are inferior to no domestic question whatever. The time has come for the people of the United States to declare themselves in favour of free seas and progressive free trade throughout the world, and by solemn manifestations to place their moral influence at the side of their successful example.

" 2. *Resolved*,—That our geographical and political position, with reference to the other States of this continent, no less than the interest of our commerce, and the development of our growing power, requires that we should hold sacred the principles involved in the Monroe doctrine.* Their bearing and import admit of no misconstruction, and should be applied with unbending rigidity.

"3. *Resolved*,—That the great highway, which nature as well as the assent of States most immediately interested in its maintenance has marked out for free communication between the Atlantic and Pacific Oceans, constitutes one of the most important achievements realized by the spirit of modern times, in the unconquerable energy of our people;

---

* The celebrated "Monroe Doctrine," upon which the pro-Slavery democracy have attempted to model the foreign policy of their country, is contained in the following two paragraphs from President Monroe's message to Congress in 1823. The Democratic party consider it now to include "non-intervention," as well as " non-colonization."

" 1. That it is impossible for the Allied Powers to extend their political system to any part of America without endangering our peace and happiness, and equally impossible, therefore, that we should behold such interference with indifference.

" 2. That the occasion has been judged proper for asserting, as a principle, in which the rights and interests of the United States are involved, that the American continents (not *continent*), by the free and independent condition which they have assumed and maintained, are henceforth not to be considered as subjects for future colonization by any other power."

and that result would be secured by a timely and efficient exertion of the control which we have the right to claim over it, and no power on earth should be suffered to impede or clog its progress by any interference with relations that it may suit our policy to establish between our Government and the Governments of the States within whose dominions it lies; we can under no circumstances surrender our preponderance in the adjustment of all questions arising out of it.

"4. *Resolved*,—That in view of so commanding an interest, the people of the United States cannot but sympathize with the efforts which are being made by the people of Central America to regenerate that portion of the Continent which covers the passage across the inter-oceanic isthmus.

"5. *Resolved*,—That the Democratic Party will expect of the next Administration, that every proper effort be made to ensure our ascendancy in the Gulf of Mexico, and to maintain permanent protection to the great outlets through which are emptied into its waters the products raised out of the soil, and the commodities created by the industry of the people of our Western valleys, and of the Union at large."

This is the solemn declaration of principles of the Democratic party of the United States—the profession of faith to which Mr. Buchanan had again to subscribe before receiving the nomination of the Cincinnati Convention and the suffrages of the electors. He has done his utmost to carry out the policy embodied in the above resolutions, and, if he have failed in making that policy triumphant, the cause of his failure is due rather to the public feeling of the northern section of the Union than to the attitude of Great Britain. By means of his creature, Senator Benjamin of Louisiana, he introduced a bill into Congress for the forced purchase of Cuba at his own valuation: this he was compelled to withdraw. The present troubles of Mexico are as much due to the machinations of his party as to the chronic anarchy of that republic, and we can never hope to see peace restored to that unhappy country whilst a Slavery president rules the destinies of the American Union. The San Juan difficulty was got up for the sole purpose of drawing off the attention of the Free States from home concerns, but the North saw through the flimsy scheme, and refused to make a trumpery island a *casus belli.*

In contradistinction to the above resolutions, we have the noble declaration of principles of the Republican party in June, 1856. The Republican Convention was held two weeks subsequently to the Democratic, and the following resolution is intended as a set-off to the foreign policy of the Slave party:—

" *Resolved,*—That the highwayman's plea, that 'might makes right,' embodied in the Ostend Circular, was in every respect unworthy of American diplomacy, and would bring shame and dishonour upon any Government or people that gave it their sanction."

Could any language be more concise, or more clearly prove that the Free North is a determined foe to all intermeddling with neighbouring States? And are we not justified in believing that when the anti-Slavery party attains to power, it will pay due respect to the law of nations, and ignore that buccaneering policy which has made the United States a byword and a reproach amongst the Governments of the earth?

THE ACT FORCING SLAVERY UPON KANSAS.

A powerful band of adherents having been formed in the Free States, and the Federal Government committed to a pro-Slavery policy, the South now began to look upon the fertile plains of the far west, as Ahab upon the vineyard of Naboth. Overland emigrants to California and Oregon had remarked the value of the Nebraska territory—a territory specially set apart by the Missouri Compromise to free labour. In nowise deterred by the sacredness of that compromise, the Slave power resolved to convert the territory into a number of Slave States; and with that object, they introduced the Kansas-Nebraska

Bill into the United States Senate. The moment was propitious. David R. Atchison, of Missouri, one of the most violent of the Slave-holding oligarchy, was President of the Senate, and Judge Douglas, the Chairman of Committee on Territories. Mr. Pierce had completed half the term of his presidential career, and professional politicians were preparing to make bids for the office soon to fall vacant. Foremost amongst these was Senator Douglas of Illinois, only too ready to pander to the South; following, in this respect, Van Buren, Webster, and Cass, and, like them, doomed to be cheated of his recompense.

In 1854, Mr. Douglas, with an eye to the next presidential nomination of the pro-Slavery party, electrified the Northern States by introducing his famous Kansas-Nebraska Bill into Congress, *abolishing the Missouri Compromise* and adding a new article to the Democratic creed, entitled " Squatter Sovereignty," meaning the sovereignty over a territory of the squatters or settlers in it. This Kansas-Nebraska Bill not merely abolished the Missouri Compromise, but, by giving *the right* of legislating to the settlers, transferred that right from, and denied it to, Congress, in whom alone it had been vested by the Constitution of the United States.

The bill was introduced into Congress, and rushed through the various stages into law at the close of the session, in order to obviate the opposition of the North. The various territorial officers, such as governor, secretary, chief justice, associate justices, attorney, marshals, &c., were immediately appointed in the name of the President of the Republic—the imbecile Mr. Franklin Pierce—by the secret junta of Southern chiefs, sometimes called "the Kitchen Cabinet," and Mr. Atchison forthwith quitted his seat in the Senate to organize the new territory of Kansas in the Slave interest. The intention of the South was to overrun the territory with settlers from the Slave districts, adopt a Slave-holding Constitution, and apply immediately for admission into the Union as a Slave State. But they counted without the North, who, for the first time in the history of the country, had become thoroughly roused, and had resolved, that *coûte que coûte*, Kansas should be a Free State.

On the 30th of May, 1854, the Territory was thrown open to emigrants, and, on the 29th of November following, the settlers proceeded to the election of a Territorial Delegate to Congress. In the meantime, secret organizations, called "blue lodges," had been formed in the adjoining Slave State of

Missouri, under the immediate supervision and direction of Senator Atchison. The Northern States, quickly discerning that this new doctrine of squatter sovereignty could be used equally well for their object as for that of the South, and taking example from what was passing in Missouri, immediately set on foot " Emigrant Aid Societies," for the purpose of assisting free labourers to reach Kansas in the speediest and cheapest mode possible. Hundreds of emigrants forthwith traversed the Northern States towards the new battle-ground of freedom. The superior numbers and greater capital of the Free North seemed to promise them an easy victory; but they ignored the determination of the South and the treachery of the President and his Cabinet. At a meeting held in Westport, Missouri, on the 29th July, 1854, a " self-defensive organization" was formed, with the avowed object of fostering the Slave interest in Kansas territory, every member swearing " to assist in removing any and all emigrants who go there under the auspices of Northern Emigrant Aid Societies."

Before we enter upon the history of Kansas and her struggles for liberty, let us once more revert to the previous outrages of the Slave power and the supineness of the North. In 1820, the Free States

had consented to an unholy compromise, delivering
up immense regions to the curse of Slavery, when
continued resistance might have saved those regions
to freedom.   In 1850, they allowed the Fugitive
Slave Bill to become law, grumbling a little, it is
true, but finally acquiescing. These two encroach-
ments only indirectly affected themselves; now they
were to learn by the bitter fruits of experience that
tyranny over the negro must eventuate in tyranny
towards themselves. And as the oppression of the
former brought the consenting white men of the North
into a more terrible bondage, so will the victory of
the latter bring about the eventual freedom of the
Slave. The masses of the Free States do not recognize this logical consequence : they labour at the
present moment for their own single interest, declaring
aloud that the Republican is " a white man's party,"
little thinking that *Slavery restriction involves Slavery
abolition*, as the greater circle includes the less.

Mr. A. H. Reeder, of Pennsylvania, was appointed
Governor of the newly organized territory.   Previous to his arrival, numerous settlements had been
formed dignified with the title of towns; Lawrence,
Topeka, Boston, Grasshopper Falls, Pawnee, &c.,
being those of the Free State party, while the pro-
Slavery men had established themselves at Kickapoo,

Doniphan, Atchison, and other spots along the Missouri river.

We shall now proceed to give a chronological history of the leading events in this Kansas struggle, feeling satisfied that nothing could more strongly portray the atrocities of Slavery than this long roll of murders and rapine. And lest it may be supposed that matters are not quite so bad as represented, we will add that these villanies have been owned to and denounced in the Senate of the United States, investigated and proved by a Congressional Investigating Committee, and hypocritically deplored by the President of the Confederation.

THE STRUGGLE FOR FREEDOM IN KANSAS.

Governor Reeder reaches Leavenworth on the 6th October, 1854, and in reply to General Pomeroy's address, pledges himself to preserve the purity of the ballot-box, and the right of free speech.

In November following, a committee of citizens of Missouri wait on the Governor to urge an immediate election of a territorial legislature; he declares that he will not be dictated to by Missourians, the people of Kansas having the right to manage their own affairs. At the election of a territorial delegate, on November 26th, organized parties of armed intruders from Missouri take possession of the polls. Out of 2,871 votes cast, it was subsequently declared, by the Congressional Investigating Committee, that 1,729 were illegal.

In February, 1855, the Territorial Census was completed. Population, 8,501, exclusive of Indians: males, 5,128; females, 3,373; minors, 3,467; of foreign birth, 409; slaves, 242; free negroes, 151; voters, 2,905. The Governor divided the territory into eighteen districts, appointed poll-officers, and ordered an election for a territorial legislature to be held on the 30th of March.

Large parties of armed intruders from Missouri take possession of the polls on the day of election, and return as members such persons as they choose. It appeared, by the investigations of the Congressional Committee, that of the 2,905 voters, named in the census roll, only 831 were found on the poll-books. Of 1,310 legal votes, 791 were given for the Free State candidates, though in many cases the Free State men were deterred from attending, or were driven from the polls by the violence of the Missouri mob, by whom were polled 4,908 illegal votes. Only four days were allowed in which to protest against the returns of the judges of elections, and in few districts could the proper formalities be attended to in season. The Governor granted certificates to all those against whom no petitions or affidavits were filed, but, as regarded the districts of Lawrence, Leavenworth, and four others, in which it was proved by witnesses that there had been illegal voting, he set aside the returns and ordered new elections to be held.

This outrage upon the rights of the people of Kansas was, shortly afterwards, confessed to publicly by Senator Atchison, in a speech to the inhabitants of his own State of Missouri. He therein used this language:—

"Well, what next? Why, an election for members of the Legislature to organize the territory must be held. What did I advise you to do then? Why, meet them on their own ground, and beat them at their own game again; and cold and inclement as the weather was, I went over with a company of men. My object in going was not to vote. I had no right to vote, unless I had disfranchised myself in Missouri. I was not within two miles of a voting place. My object in going was not to vote, but to settle a difficulty between two of our candidates; and the Abolitionists of the North said, and published it abroad, that Atchison was there with bowie-knife and revolver— and by God 'twas true. I never did go into that territory— I never intend to go into that territory—without being prepared for all such kind of cattle. Well, we beat them, and Governor Reeder gave certificates to a majority of all the members of both Houses; and then, after they were organized, as everybody will admit, they were the only competent persons to say who were, and who were not, members of the same."

The *New York Herald* substantiates the above statement by a letter which appeared in its columns shortly after the armed invasion of the territory. The *Herald's* correspondent dates from the State of Missouri, on the 20th of April, and, glorying in his shame, proceeds as follows:—

" From five to seven thousand men started from Missouri to attend the election, some to remove, but the most to return to their families, with an intention, if they liked the territory, to make it their permanent abode at the earliest moment practicable. But they intended to vote. The Missourians were, many of them, Douglas men. They were one hundred and fifty voters from this county (Brunswick), one hundred and seventy-five from Howard, one hundred from Cooper. Indeed, every county furnished its quota; and when they set out, it looked like an army. . . . They were armed. And, as there were no houses in the territory, they carried tents. Their mission was a peaceable one—to vote. . . . After the election, some one thousand five hundred of the voters sent a committee to Mr. Reeder (the Governor), to ascertain if it was his purpose to ratify the election. He answered that it was, and said the majority at an election must carry the day. But it is not to be denied that the

7

one thousand five hundred, apprehending that the Governor might attempt to play the tyrant, since his conduct had already been insidious and unjust, wore on their hats bunches of hemp. They were resolved, if a tyrant attempted to trample upon the rights of the sovereign people, to hang him."

On April the 14th, a Missouri mob destroys the press of the *Parkville* (Platte County) *Luminary*, because of the insertion in it of an article condemning the Missouri invasion, and maintaining that the people of Kansas ought to be permitted to manage their own affairs. The editor of the paper is compelled to fly for his life. At a public meeting held in the town of Leavenworth, Lecompte, Chief Justice of the territory, addresses the pro-Slavery men, and a Committee of Vigilance is appointed, by which several citizens are notified to leave, on the charge of expressing "abolition sentiments," or, in other words, a wish to make Kansas a Free State.

A band of Missouri ruffians cross the river at Leavenworth on the 17th of May, and, seizing Wm. Phillips, a lawyer, who had signed the protest against the Leavenworth election, carry him eight miles up the river to Weston, in Missouri, where they tar and feather him, ride him on a rail, and sell him at auction to a negro. He bore himself through the whole with the greatest bravery, and, returning to

Leavenworth, insisted on remaining there, though ordered to leave on peril of his life. New elections are held at Lawrence, Leavenworth, and other places, at which Free State members are chosen, except at Leavenworth, where the election is again carried by a mob from Missouri. A public meeting of the pro-Slavery party of Leavenworth and vicinity, in which two members elect of the bogus Legislature take part, " heartily endorses" the outrage on Mr. Phillips.

June 11*th.*—Governor Reeder, who had left the territory some weeks previous, for the purpose of consulting the Administration, instead of any encouragement and support towards maintaining the rights of the resident settlers, receives a letter from Secretary Marcy, charging him with irregular proceedings in the purchase of Indian lands. Having arrived at Kansas, Reeder addresses a letter to Secretary Marcy, denying these charges, and explaining the circumstances out of which they had arisen. He was one of a company formed to purchase certain districts of the Kaw half-breed lands, but for want of official sanction the purchase was not made. Mr. Reeder is soon after assaulted in his office by B. F. Stringfellow, a creature of Atchison's, on the ground of his having expressed, whilst at Washington, an unfavourable opinion of border ruffianism.

7—2

July 2nd.—The pro-Slavery Legislature assembles at Pawnee, near Fort Riley, in the interior of the territory. Mr. M. F. Conway, the only Free State man returned as elected, is unseated, and the office given to his pro-Slavery competitor. The members of the House chosen at the second election ordered by Governor Reeder, are also deprived of their seats, and the pro-Slavery Legislature passes an Act removing the seat of government to Shawnee Mission, near the Missouri border. Governor Reeder vetoes this measure as inconsistent with the Organic Act, but it is passed over his veto by a two-thirds vote. The Legislature reassembles at Shawnee Mission, and Governor Reeder, on his arrival there, finds a notice from Secretary Marcy of his intended removal. A bill having been passed and sent to the Governor, he vetoes it on the ground that the Assembly had no authority to change the place of session, which the Governor was authorized by the Organic Act to select, and delares that all subsequent proceedings were therefore void. D. Houston, the only Free State man of the Assembly, resigns his seat on the ground that not only had the Legislature been illegally elected, but that by removing from Pawnee it had nullified itself. The pro-Slavery Legislature thereupon send a memorial to Washington, containing various charges against Governor Reeder, and asking his removal.

The two Houses of the Kansas Legislature subsequently go into joint session and elect the various officers for the counties into which they had divided the territory. These officers, except justices of the peace and constables, were chosen for two years or more, many of them being residents of Missouri, and the appointment of justices of the peace and constables was given to commissioners chosen by the Legislature.

The removal of Governor Reeder is officially announced July 31st,* and the administration of the territory remains for a month in the hands of Secretary Woodson, of Arkansas, who co-operates in all things with the pro-Slavery ruffians.

August 8th. — Riotous proceedings at Atchison. Mr. J. W. B. Kelley beaten, abused, and driven from the town on the charge of being an Abolitionist. The Rev. Pardee Butler, who had condemned these proceedings, is placed on a raft and sent down the Missouri. A convention of the people of Kansas,

---

* On his return to his native State of Pennsylvania, Mr. Reeder made the following declaration in a speech delivered at the town of Easton:—"It was indeed too true that Kansas had been invaded, conquered, subjugated, by an armed force from beyond her borders, led on by a fanatical spirit, trampling under foot the principles of the Kansas Bill and the right of suffrage."

assembled at Lawrence, repudiates the authority of
the bogus Legislature, and recommends the election
of delegates on the 25th, to meet at Big Springs,
September 5th, to consider the state of affairs. The
pro-Slavery Legislature adjourned on August 30th,
after passing Acts fixing the seat of government at
Lecompton, and making it a capital offence to assist
Slaves in escaping either into the territory or out of it.
Concealing Slaves, aiding Slaves to escape, circulating
anti-Slavery publications, or denying the right to
hold Slaves in the territory, was constituted a felony,
punishable with imprisonment and hard labour during
not less than two or more than five years. Also, an
Act giving the right to vote to all persons who had
paid a poll-tax of one dollar, *whether residents or not;*
an Act requiring all voters, officers, and attorneys, to
take an oath to support the " Fugitive Slave Law "
and the proceedings of the pro-Slavery Legislature;
and an Act giving the selection of jurors to the
sheriff. They wound up their proceedings by
adopting *en masse*, without discussion, the whole
body of laws of the Slave State, Missouri.

September 1st.—Mr. Wilson Shannon, of Ohio,
assumes office as Governor of Kansas. The evening
before, in a speech at Westport, Missouri, he declared himself in favour of the obnoxious laws and

of Slavery in the territory. A Free State Convention, held at Big Springs, September 5th, repudiates these laws, nominates ex-Governor Reeder as delegate to Congress, appoints a day for holding elections (it being resolved not to vote at the election for delegates to Congress, ordered by the pro-Slavery Legislature), and passes the following resolution :—

" *Resolved*,—That the body of men who, for the last two months, have been passing laws for the people of our Territory, moved, counselled, and dictated to by the demagogues of Missouri, are to us a foreign body, representing only the lawless invaders who elected them, and not the people of the Territory. That we repudiate their action as the monstrous consummation of an act of violence, usurpation, and fraud, unparalleled in the history of the Union, and worthy only of men unfitted for the duties, and regardless of the responsibilities, of Republicans."

On the 17th, the Assembly at Topeka makes arrangements for electing delegates to a Convention, in which a State Constitution should be drawn up consonant with free labour principles, and an Executive Committee is appointed.

October 1st.—The pro-Slavery election of delegates takes place, and Whitfield is returned by 2,800 votes, polled mostly by intruders from Missouri. Stringfellow writes a letter to Alabama (a Slave State), which is published soon after in the *Mont-*

gomery Advertiser, calling for aid. Free State election of delegate on October 9th—Reeder has about 2,400 votes, and delegates to the Constitutional Convention are also elected. Collins, a Free State man, is murdered at Doniphan, on October 31st, by one Patrick Loughlin, an Irishman and pro-Slavery partisan.

November 11*th*.—The Free State Convention at Topeka complete their labours, and submit a Constitution to the people, March 4th being appointed for organizing the State Government. A "Law and Order" Convention, held at Leavenworth on the 14th (in which Shannon and the Territorial judges take part), denounces the Free State movement. 21*st*.—Murder, at Hickory Point, of Dow, a Free State man, by Coleman, who had quarrelled with him as to the ownership of a claim. Coleman flies to Westport, and puts himself under the guidance of Sheriff Jones, a pro-Slavery officer. Jones obtains from a justice of the peace of his own party, on a complaint sworn to by the murderer Coleman, a warrant, on which, with a posse of fifteen men, he arrests Branson, with whom Dow had boarded. Branson is rescued by a party of fifteen of his neighbours, including two citizens of Lawrence. Jones writes to Shannon that "an open rebellion had already commenced," and calls for 3,000 men, "to carry out the laws," and Shannon issues orders accordingly. Large numbers of Missouri ruffians array themselves as Kansas militia, and an United States arsenal in Clay County is robbed to supply them with arms. The citizens of Lawrence organize for defence, and Robinson is chosen commander, with Lane as his lieutenant.

December 3rd.—Lawrence beleaguered.—A party headed by Richardson, Shannon's Commander-in-Chief of Kansas Militia, Judge Cato, one of the Territorial judges appointed by the President, and Major Clarke, a Government Indian agent, fire upon and wantonly kill a Free State man named Thomas Barber, whilst riding unarmed on the road from Lawrence to his own house.—A treaty of peace being concluded between Shannon, Robinson, and Lane, the pro-Slavery band, mainly composed of Missourians, retires in disgust.—The Free State Constitution is subsequently endorsed by the people with little interruption, except at Leavenworth, where the election is broken up by ruffians from Missouri, and the poll-books stolen. Exclusive of Leavenworth, the vote was—for the Constitution, 1,741; against it, 46. Atchison writes the same day to Georgia (another Slave State) for aid, and his letter is soon after published in the *Atlantic Examiner.*—The jail at Leavenworth is burnt by a pro-Slavery mob on the 18th, and the rioters rescue one of their men confined in it. The *Territorial Register* printing office (the Free State paper at Leavenworth) is destroyed by a mob.

January 15th, 1856.—Election of officers under the Topeka (Free State) Constitution, when Robinson is chosen Governor. The election having been prevented on the 15th at Leavenworth by order of the Mayor, is held at Easton, twelve miles distant. A body of pro-Slavery men having attempted to steal the ballot-box, a collision ensues, in which two are wounded on either side, and one pro-Slavery man killed. Mr. E. P. Brown, a Free State man, subsequently falls into the hands of the Missouri ruffians, by whom he is barbarously murdered.—The President (Mr. Pierce), who had stated in his Annual Message, December 28th, that nothing had occurred in Kansas to warrant his interference, sends a special message to Congress, endorsing the pro-Slavery Legislature, and representing the formation of the Free State Government as an act of rebellion.

February 11th.—Proclamation of the President denouncing the State Government, and giving authority to Shannon to employ United States troops to enforce the pro-Slavery laws.

March 4th.—The State Legislature meets at Topeka, and after organizing and swearing in the Governor and other officers, adjourns to the 4th of July.—The House of Representatives at Washington, convinced of the unholy alliance between the Executive and the Slave interest, appoints a Committee of Investigation on the 19th of March, the committee being ordered to examine into the validity of the pro-Slavery Legislature and the right of its nominee, Whitfield, to a seat in Congress as delegate from Kansas.

A regiment of men, under Major Buford, enlisted in Alabama, Carolina, and Georgia, arrives in Kansas during April, for the avowed purpose of driving out the Free State men.—The Congressional Investigating Committee arrives at Lawrence on the 17th.—Arrests of Free State men are made at Lawrence by Sheriff Jones, and a company of United States dragoons.

May 5th.—Lecompte charges the Grand Jury of Douglas County, advising them to find indictments for high treason against all who had participated in organizing the Free State Government. Thus advised, the jury find indictments against Robinson, Lane, Reeder, and others. They also presented the two Lawrence newspapers and the Free State hotel as nuisances. Reeder, summoned to appear before the Grand Jury, declines to attend, on the ground

of privilege, being then in attendance before the
Congressional Committee. — Governor Robinson,
while descending the Missouri River on his way
east, is seized and detained by a mob at Lexington,
Missouri. He is afterwards sent back to Kansas,
where, with six others, he is held a close prisoner
for four months, without bail, on a charge of
treason. Reeder and Lane are also indicted, but
succeed in escaping out of the territory.—Lawrence is again beleaguered on the 13th, and many
travellers are taken prisoners, and many robberies
committed. A Free State man, of the name of
Jones, is wantonly murdered on the 19th by some
of Donaldson's ruffians, at Blanton's Bridge. In a
collision between the murderers and two or three of
Jones's friends, one of them, by name John Stuart,
is also killed. The invaders approach Lawrence in
great force. Deputy Marshal Fane rides in, and
makes certain arrests. Sheriff Jones then enters
the town, and by a promise of protection to property
obtains the surrender of the cannon and arms. This
accomplished, the army of invasion, after a speech
from Atchison (who had resigned his office of
President of the Senate at Washington, in order to
engineer Slavery into the territory), marches into
the town. The hotel is battered, blown up, and

burnt, the two printing-presses destroyed, Governor Robinson's house burnt, and all the stores and houses searched and plundered. The damages were estimated at 30,000*l.* Roving parties of Buford's men and other ruffians spread over the territory, and attempt to drive the Free State men from their homes, compelling them to take up arms in self-defence.—Fight at Potawatomie on May 26th, in which three Free State men and five invaders are killed.—Major Wilkes, of South Carolina, at the head of a party of Buford's men, arrests five of the principal citizens of Leavenworth on the 28th, and orders them to leave the city. An attempt is also made to kill the correspondent of the *Tribune,* who escapes with difficulty.—A public meeting, held at Leavenworth on the 31st, passes violent resolutions against the Free State men, and appoints a committee of safety, composed chiefly of Federal pro-Slavery officials.

June 2*nd.*—The Free State men, under Captains Brown* and Shore, attack a party of plunderers at Palmyra (fifteen miles from Lawrence), who had committed many robberies and other outrages under the lead of one Pate, of South Carolina. They take thirty-one prisoners, and recover a large quantity of plunder. 3*rd.*—Battle of Franklin. The Free State

* Lately hanged in Virginia.

men attack another party of plunderers, who had established themselves with cannon at Franklin, four miles from Lawrence; kill one, wound two, and capture the enemy's stores.—Whitfield, the late bogus delegate, having advanced into the territory at the head of a body of Missouri ruffians, is driven back by Colonel Sumner and the United States dragoons, who had previously released the prisoners taken by the Free State men. The pro-Slavery men retire, taking a prisoner as they go, named Cantril, whom they afterwards murder in cold blood. 7th.—Osawatomie sacked with great atrocities by a pro-Slavery party of one hundred and seventy men, including many of the prisoners just released by Sumner. The larger armed parties in the territory are dispersed by Sumner, but numerous outrages continue to be perpetrated by small bands of marauders; the territory, in fact, remains for three months in a state of civil war. 20th.—A company of seventeen emigrants from Chicago, on their way up the Missouri River, are robbed of their arms in the State of Missouri. On arriving at Weston, they are plundered of all their property by a mob, headed by Atchison and Stringfellow, and are sent down the river again. 21st.—Mr. Day, an Indian Agent, the only Free State Federal office-holder in the

territory, is brutally murdered by Missouri ruffians.
26th.—A number of Massachusetts emigrants, under
Dr. Cutter, are robbed near Lexington, and sent
back; and a party of Illinois emigrants undergoes
the same fate. The Rev. Mr. Strawn, their leader,
escapes, and applies to Governor Shannon, Colonel
Sumner, and Chief Justice Lecompte, for assistance
in recovering his property, but in vain.

July 4th.—The Free State Legislature, reassembled at Topeka, is forcibly dispersed by Colonel
Sumner. The Missouri River and the passage
through the State of Missouri are interdicted to Free
State emigrants, the banks of the river being guarded
by armed mobs. All steamers are stopped, and
individuals suspected to be from the North have
their trunks broken open. Many are robbed, and
turned back. In consequence of these interruptions,
the intercepted emigrants attempt a new route by
Iowa and Nebraska. Colonel Sumner, not giving
satisfaction to the Slave interest, is superseded, and
General Smith, of Louisiana, appointed in his place.

August 3rd.—At the request of the inhabitants of
Osawatomie, a body of men from Lawrence march
against a post of Georgian marauders established in
that neighbourhood. The invaders fly, and the post
is destroyed. Major Hoyt, sent from Lawrence to

remonstrate with a body of invaders under Colonel
Treadwell established at Fort Saunders on Washington Creek, twelve miles from Lawrence, is waylaid by
them on his return and brutally murdered. A party
of immigrants, led by Lane, consisting of three hundred
and twenty-four men, sixty women and children, arrive
at Kansas by the Nebraska route. Three parties
are left behind to form as many towns on the road,
and only about half the whole number reach Topeka.
12th.—Second battle of Franklin. A post of marauders established there is taken, the cannon with
which Lawrence had been battered, and large quantities of arms, and many stolen horses are recovered;
the Free State men losing one killed and six wounded.
The pro-Slavery garrison of Fort Saunders thereupon
take the alarm and fly. 14th.—Titus's fortified house
near Lecompton is battered and taken with twenty-
one prisoners, including Titus, who was wounded. (This
Titus, a violent pro-Slavery leader, subsequently joined
the filibustering expedition against Nicaragua.)

Stringfellow and Atchison issue a circular from
Westport, Missouri, on the 16th August, in which
they state that Lane had entered Kansas with an
army, that Lecompton had been taken, the dragoons
whipped, and the treason prisoners liberated, and
summon all in favour of Kansas being a Slave State

to the rescue.   Shannon orders Sedgwick, commander of the dragoons at Lecompton, to march upon Lawrence, demand the prisoners taken at Titus's house, and to fire upon the Free State men if they refused to give them up.   Sedgwick declines the enterprise as not feasible, and advises the Governor to treat with the Lawrence men.   17*th.*—Second treaty of Lawrence.   Suspension of hostilities agreed to. Shannon gives up the cannon stolen from Lawrence, and receives Titus and the other prisoners in exchange. The same day, near Leavenworth, Mr. Hopps and a teamster are murdered and scalped by a pro-Slavery party—*the former on a bet of six dollars against a pair of boots.*   The boots were given to the murderer, and he was sent off down the river.   A German, who expressed his horror at this murder, was shot dead in the street, and others manifesting similar opinions were obliged to flee.   Richardson, commander of the pro-Slavery forces, calls out the militia, under pretence of an invasion by Lane. Missouri mobs of armed men, collected under String-fellow and Atchison's proclamation, begin to assemble at Westport, Missouri.   Shannon having received notice of his removal from office, Woodson, acting governor, calls out all the militia of the territory; but as there is no territorial militia, this proclamation

8

only affords a colour of law to the organization of
armed bodies from Missouri.   A party of Georgians
plunder and break up the Quaker mission on the
road from Westport to Lawrence, and treat the
inmates with shocking barbarity.   The ruffians collected at Westport, under Atchison, advance to
Santa Fe near the border of the territory.   On the
25th, their numbers are increased to 1,150 men, rank
and file.   Organizing themselves into two regiments,
they choose Atchison commander-in-chief, and take
the name of the "Army of Law and Order in Kansas
Territory."   The same day, Woodson, at Lecompton,
issues a proclamation declaring the territory in a
state of open insurrection and rebellion.   He collects
another ruffian force there, and Lawrence is thus
blockaded on the east and west.   Atchison's army
marches upon Osawatomie, and encamps at Cedar
Creek.—A party of Free State men, principally from
Osawatomie, attack and put to flight a body of
Missouri plunderers near South Middle Creek, and,
following them up, recover next day a large drove of
stolen cattle.   Atchison's army, having encamped
the night before at Bull Creek, sends off by night a
detachment under Reid, with a piece of artillery, to
attack Osawatomie.   The defenders—some forty or
fifty men—though taken by surprise, make a vigorous

resistance. Two are killed, five wounded, and seven taken prisoners—two of whom were afterwards shot in cold blood. The mail, which had just arrived, is plundered, and thirty buildings are burnt. The ruffians reported five of their number wounded; but their loss was estimated much higher by the other party.—Lane, with 300 men, marches from Lawrence on the 30th August, to attack Atchison's camp at Bull Creek, accomplishing that day a march of forty-five miles. Woodson's militia, at Lecompton, employ this (30th) and following day in burning the houses of Free State men near that place, in presence of the United States dragoons, who do not interfere to prevent them. On the appearance of Lane, Atchison retires, and is followed till he retreats into Missouri, when Lane returns to Lawrence. Atchison's forces disperse shortly after, but agree to reassemble on the 13th of September for a new march on Lawrence.

September 1st.—The annual municipal election at Leavenworth. Captain Emory, a mail contractor or mail agent, and the leader in several previous outrages upon Free State men, enters Leavenworth at the head of a mob, chiefly from Western Missouri. Under pretence of searching for arms, they attack the house of a man named Phillips, who stands upon his defence, and, in repelling the mob, kills two of

them. They finally succeed in breaking into his
house, shoot him dead, and wound other inmates.
Many buildings are burnt, and some fifty of the
inhabitants are driven on board the *Polar Star*, and
forced to leave for St. Louis. After this, the election
takes place, without a single vote being given, as
the pro-Slavery newspapers throughout the Union
boasted, for the Free State candidates. 2*nd.*—Outrages
renewed at Leavenworth. Emory forces about a hundred more of the inhabitants to embark for St. Louis.
Many others fly from the town, and seek refuge in the
fort, three miles distant. Gen. Smith, in command at
the fort, makes no effort to put a stop to these outrages.
The communications with Lawrence being completely
interrupted, the supplies of provisions growing short,
and the messengers sent to Lecompton to communi-
cate with Woodson, the acting governor, having been
arrested and detained there, Lane marches upon
Lecompton with all his force, to demand from Woodson an explanation of his making war upon, and
burning the houses of Free State men, and to compel
the release of the Free State prisoners in his hands.
Having taken a position commanding the town, he
learns, by means of a flag of truce sent into it, and
also from Colonel Cook of the United States dragoons, who speedily appears on the field with his

whole force, that, owing to a quarrel between Woodson and some of his Missourian militia, on the subject of burning the houses of Free State men, and their refusal to being employed any longer in that business, a part of them had marched for home; whereupon Woodson had disbanded the rest of his pretended militia, and had released his prisoners. It having been agreed that these men so released should be sent home the next day under an escort of dragoons, Lane and his forces return to Lawrence.— The regular term of the Supreme Court, at which the trial of the treason prisoners was to come off, opens at Lecompton on the 8th; and at midnight the stores in Leavenworth of those inhabitants who had been driven away by Woodson, are plundered.—The district attorney not being ready to go on with the trials, the treason prisoners are released on bail (in consequence, it is supposed, of orders from Washington). The same day, Mr. Geary, appointed governor of the territory by the President, arrives at Lecompton. 11*th.*—Governor Geary assumes office, and issues a proclamation disbanding the militia called out by Woodson, and commands " all bodies of men, combined, armed, and equipped with munitions of war, without authority of the Government, instantly to disband and quit the territory." The Lawrence

forces, in obedience to this proclamation, and relying
upon the Governor's promise of protection, disband
accordingly; as does also, upon receipt of it, a body
of men under Lane, who had marched from Lawrence to attack a band of marauders fresh from plun-
dering and burning the town of Grasshopper Falls.
The same day the Missouri army reassembles, as
had been agreed at Westport, and marches into the
territory, 2,500 strong, formed into three regiments,
with five pieces of artillery.   14*th.*—The Missouri
army appears before Lawrence, where hasty pre-
parations are made for defence.   Geary, accom-
panied by the dragoons, throws himself between the
town and the invaders.   Though these men were
mostly Missourians, and were commanded by a
member elect of the Missouri Legislature, Geary
affects to treat them as Kansas militia, called out and
acting under the proclamation of Woodson!   With
difficulty, and much to the disgust of the greater part
of them, who were desperately bent on the plunder
and destruction of Lawrence, he prevails on them to
retire.   On their march home they commit many
outrages; among the rest, one of their number shoots
a cripple named Buffum, who had remonstrated
against the stealing of his horse.   Governor Geary
and Judge Cato come up shortly after, and take the

affidavit of the dying man. Geary subsequently enrols a company of 86 militia at Lawrence, for local defence, which he places under the command of Captain Walker, an active Free State partisan, whose house, near Lecompton, had been burnt by the border ruffians during the late disturbance. These militia stipulate that they shall not be employed in the enforcement of the pro-Slavery laws. Geary also enlists and takes into the United States pay, four companies of militia, composed of the floating Missourians, who are fitly placed under the command of the filibuster Titus. The regular troops, meanwhile, are principally employed as posses for Donaldson and his deputies, who make themselves very busy in arresting numerous other Free State men. These prisoners are shut up in miserable quarters, half starved, and otherwise subjected to many cruelties and indignities. Meanwhile, gangs of Missourians commit many outrages in the vicinity of Osawatomie, burning the steam saw-mill and all the remaining buildings at that place. To the application of the inhabitants for liberty to arm in self-defence, Geary returns a refusal. He soon after visits that district in person; but instead of causing the arrest of any of the Missouri marauders, he brings back a number of Free State prisoners.

October 6th.—Pro-Slavery elections for delegate
to Congress, for members of territorial Legislature,
and on the question of calling a Convention to form a
State Constitution. The Free State men refuse to
vote; many intrusive votes are thrown at Leavenworth and other towns nearest Missouri. Of the
4,276 votes cast for Whitfield, as delegate, 1,458
were polled at Leavenworth—*more than the total
population of that place.* On the question of a Convention, the vote was 2,592 for, 454 against. Of the
former number, 1,243 were cast at Leavenworth.
An emigrant train of some 500 Free State settlers,
led by Colonel Eldridge and General Pomeroy,
having entered the Territory by way of Nebraska, is
arrested by the dragoons, under orders from Governor
Geary. The arrested emigrants are very harshly
treated, robbed of a part of their arms and other
property, and marched prisoners to Lecompton,
where the Governor finds himself obliged to release
them. *13th.*—Free State Convention at Topeka. A
grand jury, packed by Sheriff Jones, and consisting
entirely of pro-Slavery men, find bills of indictment
for murder and other high crimes against more than
a hundred of the Free State prisoners. *18th.*—Trial
of Free State prisoners. Of those acquitted, the
larger part are immediately arrested on new charges,

and twenty-one are sentenced to five years' hard labour, with ball and chains. The remaining prisoners obtain a change of venue to Tecumseh. Most of them escape before trial, others are tried and acquitted. 28*th.*—Free State Convention at Big Springs.

November 1*st.*—Re-issue of the *Herald of Freedom* at Lawrence, and the Free State paper at Topeka is also revived.—Governor Geary having, at great pains and expense, obtained the arrest of Haynes, the murderer of Buffum, Lecompte, although the grand jury had found a bill against him for murder, dismisses him on the bail bond of Marshal Donaldson. The marshal, ordered to re-arrest him, refuses, and resigns his office. He is re-arrested, but set at liberty again by Lecompte, on *habeas corpus*, in consequence of which Geary demands Lecompte's removal. 29*th.*—Disbandment of Geary's militia. Titus, with most of his men, leaves for Nicaragua, on a filibustering expedition to join Walker.

December 16*th.*—In consequence of the representations made by Geary, Lecompte is removed from office, and James C. Harrison, of Kentucky, appointed in his place. Governor Geary, in his communications to the Government, declares that peace and order are completely re-established in the territory.

On the 6th of January, 1857, the Free State Legislature, under the Constitution adopted at Topeka,
met at the town of that name. Neither Governor
Robinson (the Governor elected by the Free State
men) nor Lieutenant-Governor Roberts was present,
nor did a quorum of the members appear. An
adjournment having been voted, the Legislature reassembled the next day, and a quorum of both houses
being present, they organized and appointed a committee to memorialize Congress for the admission of
Kansas as a State, under the Topeka Constitution.
Another committee was appointed to frame an election law. Both Houses having adjourned till the
next day, Marshal Pardee, who had returned from
Tecumseh with carriages and assistants, proceeded
to arrest senators and representatives, until he had as
many as his vehicles could carry. No resistance was
made to these arrests, the prisoners going peaceably
with the marshal to Tecumseh. When the Legislature met the next morning (January 8th) both
bodies were without presiding officers, and without
quorums ; the president of the senate, and also
the speaker of the House, being prisoners at Tecumseh. The remaining members of the two Houses
met, however, in joint session, and adopted a memorial to Congress for the admission of the State of

Kansas under the Topeka Constitution; after which, by joint resolution, they took a recess till the second Tuesday in June. The prisoners were taken before Judge Cato, at Tecumseh, and bound over to appear at the June term of his court.

Shortly after, the Territorial pro-Slavery Legislature, composed of the former council, and a new House, met at Lecompton, and elected delegates to a Convention, which was to be held on the first Monday in September. This Act was vetoed by Governor Geary, but was passed over his head. Meanwhile, the House of Representatives at Washington had passed a bill, 98 to 79, declaring void all the enactments of this Territorial Legislature, on the ground set forth in the preamble, that they were " cruel and oppressive;" and that " the said Legislature was not elected by the legal voters of Kansas, but was forced upon them by non-residents, in violation of the Organic Act of the territory." But not only did this bill fail in the Senate; the partisans of Lecompte were strong enough in that body to prevent the confirmation of the chief justice nominated by President Pierce to succeed him; so that Lecompte, who had never been actually dismissed, still held on to his office. *In this state of affairs, Geary, finding himself abandoned at Washing-*

ton, without power in the Territory, his very life in danger, and anticipating no support from the Administration of Mr. Buchanan, resigned his office, and left for home.

A State convention of the Free State men of Kansas, held at Topeka on the 11th of March, resolved not to take any part in the election ordered by the pro-Slavery Legislature. The ground of this decision was two-fold: first, a disinclination to recognize the bogus Legislature in any way; and secondly, the probability that the Free State men would be cheated and overborne by invaders, if they attempted to vote—the whole machinery of election being in the hands of their opponents. The Convention also voted an address to the people of the United States, setting forth the wrongs to which they had been, and still were, subjected.

As successor to Geary, President Buchanan appointed Robert J. Walker, of Mississippi, giving him as secretary, F. P. Stanton, of Tennessee. To most of the offices of profit in the territory, Mr. Buchanan appointed persons who had been very conspicuous for acts of violence perpetrated upon Free State men.

The census of voters ordered by the Territorial Legislature was very imperfectly taken. Some counties were omitted altogether, and in others a large part of the Free State men were overlooked. Immigration was now pouring rapidly into Kansas; but none of those who arrived after the 1st of April were enrolled on the list of voters. The indictments for treason against Governor Robinson, and others, were finally disposed of on the 11th of May, the prosecuting officer entering a *nolle prosequi.*

Stanton (who preceded Walker, and acted as Governor for some weeks), by his speeches in the territory, and Governor Walker, on his way thither, laboured to secure the confidence of the Free State men, and strongly urged them to take a part in the approaching election for members of a constitutional convention. The Free State men were willing to have done so, if they could have had any guarantees for a fair election; but these the new officials were unable to give. The reply was: " We have no power to interfere. You must obey the territorial (pro-Slavery) laws, and vote as they direct." These objections on the part of the Free State men were further met by reiterated assurances that the people of Kansas should have an opportunity for a full and solemn expression of their will upon any constitution that might be framed by the Convention. In most of the counties south of the Kansas River, and which were inhabited by Free State men, there were no territorial officers, and no attempt had been made to take the census. The Act provided not only for the registration of voters, but for a census of the entire population; in half of these counties, however, in which the registry of voters was made out, the census of inhabitants had been omitted.

In the apportionment based upon this census, four or five counties, from which there were no returns, were classed with other counties, and so included; but no less than fifteen counties, comprising nearly half the population of the territory, were left out altogether. It was even stated, that in six of the counties included in the returns, no census had actually been taken; the names and numbers being copied from the old poll-books of elections, at which no Free State men had voted. Shortly after the publication of this apportionment (the end of May), Governor Walker arrived in the territory. The Topeka Free State Legislature reassembled on the 9th of June, and this time they were 'allowed to go on without interruption. At a Free State Convention, held about the same time, a resolution was adopted, disowning the Territorial Government, and declaring the admission of the territory into the Union, *under the Topeka Constitution*, to be the only method of adjusting the existing difficulties. The

Convention also urged the completion of the State organization. The Free State Legislature passed an Act for an election of officers in August, but they declined taking any steps for the organization of cities and counties, as desired by the Convention, lest it might bring them into conflict with the territorial authorities. Provision, however, was made for taking a State census.

In spite of all the efforts of Governor Walker, the Free State men adhered to their resolution of taking no part in the bogus constitutional election, which came off on the 15th of June, and at which only about 2,000 votes out of 9,000 were thrown. At the municipal election of Leavenworth, a few days subsequent, the Free State voters rallied in force, and elected their entire ticket by a decided majority. The people of Lawrence, about the same time, carried out a project they had long entertained, of setting up a municipal government of their own. On the 13th of July they held a city election, under a charter which had been agreed upon at a public meeting. This proceeding, however, was taken in high dudgeon by Governor Walker. He fulminated a proclamation against the people of Lawrence, as having committed, or being about to commit, an act of rebellion, and immediately detached a body of troops to encamp near by, to hold the rebellious citizens in awe, and to prevent them from acting in a municipal capacity. On the 15th of July, a new Convention of the Free State men met at Topeka. The returns of the State census, though imperfect, showed a population of near 70,000. Nominations were made for the State election, which was held on the 3rd of August, without any of the interruption which had been threatened. Ever since his arrival, Governor Walker had continued to be very urgent with the Free State men to come forward and take a share in the October territorial election, and a decided inclination in favour of that course was exhibited by many of the friends of Kansas out of the Territory. Walker alleged that, in consequence of the alteration of the law at the last session of the Territorial Legislature, the payment of the tax, hitherto insisted upon as a qualification for voting, would no longer be required. Judge Cato, however, gave a written opinion the other way. Nor was the apportionment of the members such as to inspire any great hope of fair play. Sixteen Free State counties, containing nearly half the population of the territory, were not allowed a single representative in either branch of the Legis-lature. Ten out of the thirteen members of the Council, and twenty-nine out of the thirty-nine representatives, were to be chosen in districts, some part of which touched on the Missouri border, an arrangement apparently made with a particular view to the convenience of intrusive voters from Missouri. Under the Act appointing the election, the Governor was to make the apportionment on the basis of the census of voters, and if he omitted to do it within a certain period, the duty was to devolve on the presiding officers of the two branches of the preceding Territorial Legislature. The time limited expired before Walker's arrival in the Territory, and, as he alleged, before he knew of the existence of the Act. The imperfect census of voters, in which most of the Free State counties on the south side of the Kansas River had been totally omitted, furnished some colour for leaving these counties out of the apportionment; but of the singular arrangement of the districts to favour the convenience of voters from Missouri, no explanation was given. Governor Walker freely admitted the unfairness of this apportionment, but he still strongly urged the Free State men to vote, assuring them of his intention to protect the polls against any intrusion from Missouri or elsewhere. Thus pressed by the Governor and by their friends outside the Territory, the Free State men, or a part of them, were inclined to try the experiment; and at a Con-

9

vention, held at Grasshopper Falls on the 27th of August, it was resolved so to do.

Both parties now devoted their energies to that election, which, notwithstanding the unfairness of the apportionment, and the restriction of the right of voting to those registered, resulted in a decided triumph for the Free State men. They polled about 7,600 votes, to about 3,700 of the other party, elect-Parrott their candidate for Territorial delegate, nine out of the thirteen Councilmen, and twenty-seven out of the thirty-nine Representatives. An attempt was indeed made to alter the complexion of the Legislature by means of a false return sent in from the Oxford precinct in Johnson County. This return was a manuscript roll fifty feet long, containing the names of 1,624 persons, who were represented to have voted at the Oxford precinct—*a place containing eleven houses.* If admitted, by transferring from the Free State to the pro-Slavery side three Councilmen and eight representatives for the district of which this precinct formed a part, it would have changed the party character of the Legislature, though still leaving the Free State men the delegate in Congress, and a decided majority of the popular vote. But the fabricated character of this pretended return was too manifest. *The signatures of the three Judges attesting*

the validity of the election were all in the same hand-
writing, and the names of pretended voters were, as it
afterwards appeared, copied in alphabetical order from
a Cincinnati Directory. There were also serious
defects of form, and this return was rejected by the
Governor, as also another of a similar character from
McGee County. The refusal of Walker to become
a party to this fraud, was by no means satisfactory
to the parties who would have been elected by it.
They procured from Judge Cato an order to Walker
to show cause why a writ of mandamus should not
be issued, forcing him to give a certificate of election
to the bogus candidates. Walker replied to this
document by denying the jurisdiction of Cato, claiming an appeal from his decision if in favour of that
jurisdiction, and declining beforehand, even though
he should be imprisoned for contempt, to obey any
order which the Judge might issue. The pro-Slavery
Convention having reassembled, proceeded to complete their Constitution. Into the body of the Constitution a provision on the subject of Slavery was
inserted, as follows :—

" SLAVERY.

" Sec. 1.—The right of property is before and higher than
any Constitutional sanction, and the right of the owner of
a Slave to such Slave and its increase is the same, and as

inviolable, as the right of the owner of any property whatever.

" Sec. 2.—The Legislature shall have no power to pass laws for the emancipation of Slaves without the consent of the owners, or without paying their owners, previous to emancipation, a full equivalent in money for the Slaves so emancipated. They shall have no power to prevent emigrants to the State from bringing with them such persons as are deemed Slaves by the laws of any one of the States or Territories, so long as any persons of the same age or description shall be continued Slaves by the laws of this State; *provided* that such person or Slave be the *bonâ-fide* property of such emigrant; *and provided also* that laws may be passed to prohibit the introduction of Slaves into the State who have committed high crimes in other States or Territories. They shall have power to pass laws to permit the owners of Slaves to emancipate them, saving the rights of creditors, and preventing them from becoming a public charge. They shall have power to oblige the owners of Slaves to treat them with humanity, to provide for their necessary food and clothing, to abstain from all injuries to them, extending to life or limb, and, in case of neglect or refusal to comply with the direction of such laws, to have such Slave or Slaves sold for the benefit of the owner or owners."

This last provision, and this provision alone, it was finally determined by a close vote to submit to the registered electors. For this purpose, by the means of a schedule annexed to the Constitution, an election was to be held on the 21st of December. The ballots cast were to be indorsed either " Constitution with Slavery," or " Constitution with no Slavery." Thus to have the privilege of voting " no Slavery," it was still made necessary to vote for the Constitution; besides which, all persons offering to vote, must, if challenged, " take an oath to support the Constitution if adopted."

This schedule, as if with a direct view of superseding the Territorial Legislature and Congressional delegate elect, further provided that the Constitution should be in force, " after its ratification by the people " (without waiting for the approval of Congress), and that a State election should be held on the first Monday in January, 1858, for the choice of Governor, Lieutenant-Governor, Secretary of State, Auditor, State Treasurer, and Members of the Legislature, and also a Member of Congress. It also provided (as if to deprive the Territorial Legislature of any power of acting) that all laws in force, not repugnant to the Constitution, shall continue until altered, amended, or repealed, by a Legislature assembled under the provisions of the Constitution; and that all officers, civil or military, under the authority of the Territory of Kansas, shall continue to hold and exercise their respective offices, until

superseded by the authority of the State, the first
meeting of the State Legislature to take place upon
the issue of a proclamation by the President of the
Convention upon the receipt of official information
that "Congress has admitted Kansas into the Union."
A provision was also inserted preventing any amendment previous to the year 1864, and then only upon
the concurrence of two-thirds of the members of
both Houses, and "a majority of all the citizens of
the State."

This proceeding, as might have been expected,
produced the greatest excitement in Kansas. Governor Walker condemned it in the most decided terms.
He hastened at once to Washington, but before his
arrival there, the Lecompton scheme had already
received the approval of the President and his
Cabinet.

Meanwhile, Governor Walker was superseded,
and Governor Denver, a commissioner of the land
office, appointed in his stead. Secretary Stanton,
acting Governor in Walker's absence, called a special
session of the newly elected Territorial Legislature,
in which the Free State men had a majority, and
they passed an Act submitting the Lecompton Constitution to a vote of the people, to be taken on the
same day with the Lecompton election. At the

beginning of the year the Legislature, under the
Topeka Constitution, many of whose members were
also members of the Territorial Legislature, met at
Topeka, their object being merely to keep up the
State organization.

At the election of the 4th January, a majority of
10,226 votes was cast against the Lecompton Constitution. The result of the Lecompton State election long remained in doubt. It was understood
that a little over 6,000 votes (a large part of the
Free State men not voting) had been given for both
sets of candidates for State officers; but, according
to Calhoun's * figuring, the pro-Slavery men were
chosen. It was also understood that the Free State
men, of whom a large part had voted for members
of the Legislature, had a decided majority in both
branches of that body ; but all depended upon
Leavenworth County, the returns for some districts
of which had been falsified on their way to Calhoun,
and as he kept these returns to himself, and refused
to certify to any one's election till Congress had first
acted on the question by admitting Kansas into the
Union, the matter long remained in doubt. It was

---

* John Calhoun, a violent pro-Slavery partisan, was appointed
by the Administration of Mr. Buchanan to office in Kansas, and
did what lay in his power to make that territory a Slave State.

generally understood that if Kansas was admitted, Calhoun would cook up the returns so as to produce a pro-Slavery State Government and Legislature.

In spite of this renewed and unequivocal indication of the repugnance of the majority of the people of Kansas to the Lecompton Constitution, the President still adhered to the policy of forcing Kansas into the Union under that Constitution. A Bill to that effect was introduced into Congress. Senator Douglas, falling back upon his doctrine of popular sovereignty, refused to support it; and though it passed the Senate, in spite of every exertion of executive power, it was rejected in the House. Some of the bolters were bought over, others were half bought over, so that finally the Bill passed, but only with a provision submitting the question of admission or not to a vote of the people of Kansas, who were also offered a large bribe in lands, to come into the Union under the Lecompton Constitution.

It was still further attempted to bribe the people of Kansas by an issue of certificates to a majority of Free State men as members elect of both branches of the Legislature; but they scornfully rejected both bribes and threats, and at the election held on the 3rd of August, 1858, by 10,000 majority trampled the Lecompton Constitution under their feet.

PROCEEDINGS IN CONGRESS UPON THE KANSAS
TROUBLES.

Having thus given an unbroken narrative of the
misfortunes inflicted upon the men of the North in
their efforts to make Kansas a Free State, we shall
now proceed to relate what measures had been proposed for their benefit in Congress, by the anti-
Slavery Senators and Representatives.

The citizens of the North, roused by the efforts of
the Slave oligarchy and the Administration of Mr.
Pierce to force Slavery upon Kansas, carried the
elections against the Democracy in nearly all the
Free States, and returned a majority of members
to the House of Representatives for the Thirty-fourth
Congress. This majority, however, was scarcely a
working one, being composed of 117 Opposition
Members to 116 Administration. The first step in
organizing the House was to elect a Speaker, and
the contest lasted from the 3rd of December, 1855,
to the 2nd of February of the following year; Mr.
Nathaniel P. Banks of Massachusetts being finally
elected by a majority of three votes over his competitor, Mr. William Aiken, of South Carolina,—
the largest Slaveholder in the Southern States.

During the Session, Mr. Grow, of Pennsylvania, introduced the following measure into the House of Representatives, on behalf of the Free State Party :—

"A BILL FOR THE RELIEF OF KANSAS.

"*Whereas* the President of the United States transmitted to the House by message a printed pamphlet purporting to be the laws of the Territory of Kansas, passed at Shawnee Mission, in said Territory ; *and whereas* unjust and unwarrantable test-oaths are prescribed by said laws as a qualification for voting or holding office in said Territory; *and whereas* the Committee of Investigation sent by the House of Representatives to Kansas report that said Legislature was not elected by the legal voters of Kansas, but was forced upon them by non-residents, in violation of the organic Act of the Territory, and, having thus usurped legislative power, it enacted cruel and oppressive laws : Therefore,

"*Be it enacted, &c.*, that all rules or regulations purporting to be laws, or in the form of law, adopted at Shawnee Mission, in the Territory of Kansas, by a body of men claiming to be the Legislative Assembly of said Territory, and all legal acts and proceedings whatsoever of said Assembly, are hereby declared invalid and of no binding force or effect.

"Sec. 2.—*And be it further enacted*, that the Governor of said Territory shall as soon as practicable, by public proclamation, fix the time and places for an election of members of the Legislative Assembly, appoint in each district three competent persons to superintend the election therein, under such rules and regulations as he shall direct, and shall prescribe the mode and manner for the return thereof.

" Sec. 3.—*And be it further enacted*, that any person offering to vote at said election, whose vote shall be challenged, shall, in addition to the qualifications for voting fixed in the Act of Congress organizing the Territory, prove by his own oath that he is a *bonâ-fide* settler of said Territory, and by the oath of at least two legal voters that he is, and has been, for one month immediately preceding, an actual resident of said Territory, and for fifteen days a resident of the election district where he offers to vote.

" Sec. 4.—*And be it further enacted*, that if any person, not being an actual inhabitant or resident of the said Territory, shall cast his vote at any election which may be held in the said Territory by authority of law, such person so offending shall, on conviction thereof in any criminal court, be punished by fine, not less than twenty dollars, nor more than one hundred dollars, and imprisonment, not less than two months, nor more than six months.

" That if any person or persons shall come into any election district of said Territory in armed and organized bodies, for the purpose of participating in, disturbing, controlling, or voting at any election held, or to be held, under the authority of law therein, such person or persons so offending, shall, on conviction thereof in any criminal court, be punished by a fine of not less than one hundred dollars, and not exceeding five hundred dollars, and imprisonment for a term not less than three months, and not exceeding one year.

" Sec. 5.—*And be it further enacted*, that if any person

being a member of any such armed and organized body as described in the preceding section, or connected therewith, and a non-resident of the said Territory, shall vote at any election which may be held in the said Territory by authority of law, he shall, on conviction thereof, be punished by a fine of not less than one hundred dollars, and not exceeding five hundred dollars, and imprisonment for a term of not less than six months and not more than two years.

" Sec. 6.—*And be it further enacted*, that any judge of election who shall wilfully and knowingly allow any vote to be polled in violation of the fourth and fifth sections of this Act, shall, on conviction thereof, be punished by a fine of not less than fifty dollars, nor more than three hundred dollars, and imprisonment for a term of not less than six months nor more than one year.

" That all offences under this Act may be prosecuted by indictment in any criminal court having jurisdiction of felonies or misdemeanors committed in said Territory.

" All laws, rules, or regulations inconsistent with the provisions of this Act are hereby declared null and void."

This Bill was brought to an issue in the Lower House on the 17th of February, 1857, and carried by a majority of nineteen; the numbers being— for the Bill, 98; against it, 79. *Every member who voted with the majority was from the Free States*, not a single representative from the South acting with them; clearly establishing the fact that the Slave interest had resolved to make Kansas a Slave State, and that the North was equally determined to make it free.

The Bill was carried up to the Senate on the 19th of the same month, and after being read the first and second times, the Senators from Virginia and Missouri proposed to refer it, the first to the Committee on Territories, the second to the Judiciary Committee. Senator Adams of Mississippi proposed to let it lie quietly upon the table, without further notice, and the motion was carried by thirty to twenty. Eight Senators from Free States voted with the majority, thus treacherously giving up Kansas to the despotism of Slavery; but of those eight, only two retain their seats in the Senate, the others having been ousted by indignant Northern legislatures, and themselves and prospects consigned " to the tomb of the Capulets," where the other two will shortly join them.

Mr. Buchanan had succeeded Mr. Pierce as chief magistrate of the Confederation, but the oppressed inhabitants of Kansas quickly discovered they had merely exchanged King Log for King Stork. The determination became more manifest than ever on the part of the new Administration, to force Slavery upon the territory, and the dragoons quartered therein, under the new President's orders, made it appear as though the entire country were in a state of siege.

Towards the close of the session, the following resolution was unanimously adopted by the Republican Members of Congress, and subsequently endorsed by all the Northern press not under the control of the Administration:—

"*Resolved,*—That we, the Republican members of the House, deem this a proper occasion to re-affirm our adherence to the principles announced by the Republican National Convention held at Philadelphia in June, 1856" (to which we shall hereafter refer), "and we will continue our opposition to any administration that does not practically enforce those doctrines ; that we will resist, by all constitutional means, the recent attempts of the judicial and executive departments of the Government" (referring to the Dred Scott decision of the Supreme Court of the Union, to which we shall also hereafter revert) "to nationalize the sectional institution of Slavery ; that we regard the acts in Kansas of the present" (Mr. Buchanan's) "and the last" (Mr. Pierce's) "National Administrations as a continued series of frauds and outrages, now attempted to be culminated by forcing upon the people of that territory a State Constitution, framed by persons not elected by them—one which was not submitted to them, and is known to be offensive to a great majority of them, and made in direct violation even of their own repeated and solemn pledges that the people should be permitted to form and regulate their own institutions in their own way. We will resist such outrages upon popular rights, and, in doing so, invoke the support of the people of the United States, without distinction of party."

It will be remembered that the scheme for rendering the territory of Kansas a Slave State, entitled the *Lecompton Constitution*, had received the approval of Mr. Buchanan and his Cabinet. Before, however, it could become law, it must pass through Congress; and in February, 1858, the following Bill was introduced into the Senate by Mr. Green, of Missouri:—

THE LECOMPTON BILL.

" *Whereas* the people of the territory of Kansas did, by a Convention of Delegates called and assembled at Lecompton, September 4th, 1857, form for themselves a Constitution and State Government, which said Convention having asked the admission of the territory into the Union as a State on an equal footing with the original States,

" *Be it enacted by the Senate and House of Representatives of the United States of America in Congress assembled*, that the State of Kansas shall be, and is hereby declared to be, one of the United States of America, and admitted into the Union on an equal footing with the original States, in all respects whatever," &c. &c.

Senator Crittenden, of Kentucky, moved, as an

amendment to or substitute for the above, that the so-called Lecompton Constitution be first submitted to the people of Kansas, and, if approved, that the President should admit the new State by proclamation; if rejected, the citizens of the territory should be permitted to form a new constitution. This motion was defeated—yeas 24, noes 34. Senator Green's motion was then put and carried by a majority of eight.

Read in the Lower House for the first time, on the 1st of April, the Bill was thrown out by a majority of 42, the numbers being—in favour of the Bill, 95; against it, 137. Mr. Montgomery, of Pennsylvania, then proposed a substitute similar to Senator Crittenden's rejected motion, whereupon Mr. Quitman, of Mississippi, moved, as an amendment, the Bill sent down from the Senate, omitting the following clause,—" That the people shall have the right at all times to alter or amend the constitution in such manner as they think proper." This amendment was negatived by a majority of 88, but Mr. Montgomery's motion was adopted by 120 to 112. It was as follows:—

" Section 1. *Be it enacted*, *&c.*, that the State of Kansas be, and is hereby, admitted into the Union on an equal footing with the original States in all respects whatever;

but inasmuch as it is greatly disputed whether the Constitution framed at Lecompton on the 7th day of November last, and now pending before Congress, was fairly made, or expressed the will of the people of Kansas, this admission of her into the Union as a State is here declared to be upon this fundamental condition precedent, namely, that the said constitutional instrument shall be first submitted to a vote of the people of Kansas, and assented to by them, or a majority of the voters, at an election to be held for the purpose; and as soon as such assent shall be given, and duly made known, by a majority of the Commissioners herein appointed, to the President of the United States, he shall announce the same by proclamation; and thereafter, and without any further proceedings on the part of Congress, the admission of the said State of Kansas into the Union upon an equal footing with the original States, in all respects whatever, shall be complete and absolute. At the said election the voting shall be by ballot, and by indorsing on his ballot, as each voter may please, ' for the Constitution,' or ' against the Constitution.' Should the said constitution be rejected at the said election by a majority of votes being cast against it, then, and in that event, the inhabitants of said territory are hereby authorized and empowered to form for themselves a constitution and State Government, by the name of the State of Kansas, according to the Federal Constitution, and to that end may elect delegates to a convention as hereinafter provided," &c. &c.

The Senate refused to agree to this amendment by a vote of 34 to 22, whereupon the House of

Representatives sent it back to them for reconsideration. The majority in the Senate, determined to force Slavery upon the territory, insisted, and demanded a committee of conference. Mr. Montgomery then moved that the House hold to its vote, and proposed the previous question. This was lost by the casting vote of the Speaker, James L. Orr, of South Carolina. A Democratic member from the North thereupon moved that the House do agree to a committee of conference, and that the Speaker should appoint the members upon it. The yeas and nays tied, 108 to 108, and the Speaker gave his casting vote in the affirmative, and appointed two Administration men and one Republican. A similar choice was made in the Senate, so that there were four out of six on the committee adverse to Kansas entering the Union with a free constitution.

The above committee made its report on the 23rd of April, 1858, two of their number dissenting, and on the 30th of the month this report was adopted by both branches of Congress, and it became law. It is as follows:—

AN ACT FOR THE ADMISSION OF THE STATE OF KANSAS INTO THE UNION.

" *Whereas* the people of the Territory of Kansas did, by a convention of delegates assembled at Lecompton on the 7th day of November, 1857, for that purpose, form for themselves a constitution and State Government, which constitution is republican ; and *whereas*, at the same time and place, said convention did adopt an ordinance, which said ordinance asserts that Kansas, when admitted as a State, will have an undoubted right to tax the lands within her limits belonging to the United States, and proposes to relinquish said asserted right if certain conditions set forth in said ordinance be accepted and agreed to by the Congress of the United States; and *whereas*, the said constitution and ordinance have been presented to Congress by order of said convention, and admission of said Territory into the Union thereon as a State requested; and *whereas*, said ordinance is not acceptable to Congress, and it is desirable to ascertain whether the people of Kansas concur in the changes in said ordinance, hereinafter stated, and desire admission into the Union as a State, as herein proposed; Therefore,

"*Be it enacted, &c.*, that the State of Kansas be, and is hereby, admitted into the Union on an equal footing with the original States, in all respects whatever, but upon this fundamental condition precedent, namely, that the question of admission, with the following proposition in lieu of the ordinance framed at Lecompton, be submitted to a vote of the people of Kansas, and assented to by them, or a majority of the voters voting at an election to be held for that purpose, namely, that the following propositions be, and the same are hereby, offered to the people of Kansas for acceptance or rejection, which, if accepted, shall be obligatory on the United States and upon the said State of Kansas, to wit:"

(Here follow sections relating to grants of land for public schools, a State university, and public buildings; also in reference to salt-springs, and the making of public roads, and internal improvements, and providing that the future State should never tax the lands or property of the Federal Government within its confines. These conditions were annexed to the pro-Slavery Lecompton Constitution, and the people of the territory would, after all, have to consent to that obnoxious instrument, or remain out of the Union.) The Act then continues:—

"At the said election the voting shall be by ballot, and by indorsing on his ballot, as each voter may be pleased, 'proposition accepted,' or 'proposition rejected.' Should a majority of the votes cast be for 'proposition accepted,' the President of the United States, as soon as the fact is duly made known to him, shall announce the same by proclamation; and thereafter, and without any further proceedings on the part of Congress, the admission of the State of Kansas into the Union upon an equal footing with the original States, in all respects whatever, shall be complete and absolute, &c. &c. But should a majority of the votes cast be for 'proposition rejected,' it shall be deemed and held that the people of Kansas do not desire admission into Union with said constitution" (the pro-Slavery one) "under the conditions set forth in said proposition: and in that event the people of said territory are hereby authorized and empowered to form for themselves a constitution and State Government, by the name of the State of Kansas, according to the Federal Constitution, and may elect delegates for that purpose *whenever, and not before, it is ascertained by a census duly and legally taken that the population of said Territory equals or exceeds the ratio of representation required for a member of the House of Representatives of the Congress of the United States ;* and whenever thereafter such delegates shall assemble in Convention, they shall first determine by a vote, whether it is the wish of the people of the proposed State to be admitted into the Union at that time ; and if so, shall proceed to form a constitution, and take all necessary steps for the establishment of a State Government, in conformity with the Federal Constitution, subject to such limitations and restrictions, as to the mode and manner of its approval or ratification by the people of the proposed State, as they may have prescribed by law, and shall be entitled to admission into the Union as a State under such constitution, thus fairly and legally made, *with or without Slavery,* as said condition may prescribe," &c.

The Administration of Mr. Buchanan had thus managed to effect, that if the people of Kansas would consent to doom themselves to Slavery institutions, they might forthwith enter the Union with their then population ; but, if they preferred freedom in its only true sense, they must then wait several years, until, in fact, their population should reach 93,340. The Act was submitted to the vote of the people of the territory on the first Monday in August, 1858, when the free men, the representatives of liberty, carried the day against the pro-Slavery Constitution by an overwhelming majority of 9,513; the numbers being—for the Lecompton measure, and immediate admission into the Union, 1,788; against it, and in favour of Kansas becoming a Free State, 11,301.

Thus ended a conflict which had lasted for years, and in which oceans of blood and treasure had been spent. The pro-Slavery party, that had dominated the Union since its establishment, saw themselves, for the first time, defeated, though backed by all the powers and terrors of the Central Government. The floating, unorganized, anti-Slavery sentiments of the Northern States concentrated themselves upon the impending issue, and gave birth to the Republican party, which will shortly control the destinies of the country, and, finally, obliterate Slavery from the North American Continent.

If this glorious struggle for freedom had taken place in Naples, Kamschatka, or Thibet, Englishmen would have watched the shifting fortunes of the scene with breathless interest. But because it passed amongst our own race and kindred—because not foreigners were concerned, but men calling Great Britain the " Mother Country"—men, speaking the same language—men, whose constitution and laws are based upon our own, and whose very prejudices are ours—because, in fine, our former colonies were sacrificing sons and fathers and brothers to rid their country of the damning curse planted on it by ourselves, we cared little for the result. Are we Englishmen really lovers of liberty, or do we only sympathize where there is a chance of interfering to benefit ourselves? Shall it always be sneeringly asked—" Doth England profess liberty for nought?"

THE DRED SCOTT DECISION.

' In tracing the assumptions of the Slave power, we are compelled for their better elucidation, to treat each particular case separately, though by so doing we sacrifice their continuity. The celebrated decision of the Supreme Court of the United States in the action Dred Scott *v.* John F. A. Sandford was pronounced upon the 6th of March, 1857. The judgment took the Union by surprise, and whilst it astonished the North, it was hailed with triumph by the Slave States. We must premise that the nine judges of the Court are appointed for life by the Administration, and, consequently, the majority is inclined towards Slavery.

The Dred Scott case grew out of a simple action for assault and battery. The declaration of the plaintiff alleged three assaults upon himself, his wife, and their two children, and the defendant pleaded "not guilty," and a justification that the parties above mentioned were his negro Slaves. The case was tried in the State of Missouri, during the month of May, 1854, and the jury gave a verdict for the plaintiff, upon the following agreed facts :—

"In the year 1834, the plaintiff was a negro Slave belonging to Dr. Emerson, a surgeon in the army of the United States, who, in that year, took him from the State of Missouri to the military post at Rock Island, in the State of Illinois, and held him there as a Slave until the month of April or May, 1836, when he removed him to the military post at Fort Snelling, situate on the west bank of the Mississippi River, in the territory known as Upper Louisiana, acquired by the United States of France, and north of the latitude of thirty-six degrees thirty minutes north, and north of the State of Missouri. Dr. Emerson held the plaintiff in Slavery, at Fort Snelling, from the last-mentioned date, until 1838.

"In the year 1835, Harriet, who is named in the second count of the plaintiff's declaration, was the negro Slave of Major Taliaferro, who belonged to the army of the United States. In that year, Major Taliaferro took her to Fort Snelling, and kept her there as a Slave until the year 1836. He then sold her as a Slave, at Fort Snelling, unto Dr. Emerson, who held her in Slavery there until 1838.

"In the year 1836, the plaintiff and Harriet, at Fort Snelling, with the consent of Dr. Emerson, who then claimed to be their master and owner, intermarried and took each other for husband and wife. Eliza and Lizzie, named in the third count of the plaintiff's declaration, are the fruit of that marriage. Eliza is about fourteen years old, and was born on board the steam-boat *Gipsey*, north of the north line of the State of Missouri, and upon the river Mississippi. Lizzie is about seven years old, and was born in the State of Missouri, at the military post called Jefferson Barracks.

" In the year 1838, Dr. Emerson removed the plaintiff, Harriet, and their daughter Eliza, from Fort Snelling to the State of Missouri, where they have ever since resided.

" Before the commencement of this suit, Dr. Emerson sold and conveyed the plaintiff, Harriet, Eliza, and Lizzie as Slaves to the defendant, who has ever since claimed to hold them as Slaves.

" At the times mentioned in the plaintiff's declaration, the defendant, claiming to be the owner as aforesaid, laid his hands upon the plaintiff, Harriet, Eliza, and Lizzie, and imprisoned them, doing, in this respect, however, no more than what he might lawfully do if they were of right his Slaves at such times.

" Dred Scott brought suit for his freedom, in the Circuit Court of St. Louis County, when there was a verdict and judgment in his favour," &c. &c.

The case was, thereupon, transferred on writ of error to the Supreme Court of the United States. Denuding the question of minor or extraneous matter, there were two main issues before the

Court,—firstly, the rights of the coloured man; secondly, the rights of the white man; but these points involved the following:—the meaning and intention of the United States Constitution; the constitutionality of the Missouri Compromise; and the rights reserved in the Constitution to each individual State in the Confederation, as a separate and distinct sovereignty.

The nine judges did not pronounce judgment upon the question of coloured citizens of any State being entitled to citizenship of the United States. But the Chief Justice and one of the Judges (both of them natives of Slave States) gave the following extraordinary opinion, and we may, thereon, estimate the value set upon the unfortunate descendants of the African race in the Southern portions of the Confederation.

" In the opinion of the Court, the legislation and histories of the times, and the language used in the Declaration of Independence, show that neither the class of persons who had been imported as Slaves, nor their descendants, whether they had become free or not, were then acknowledged as a part of the people, nor intended to be included in the general words used in that memorable instrument. They had, for more than a century, been regarded as beings of an inferior order, and altogether unfit to associate with the white race, either in social or political relations; *and so far inferior, that they had no rights which the white man was bound to respect;* and that the negro might justly and lawfully be reduced to Slavery for his benefit."

" No rights which the white man was" *or is* "bound to respect." The Declaration of Independence defines the rights of men (these two Judges declare "men" to mean only men *who are not Africans or their descendants*) as " life, liberty, and the pursuit of happiness." Now we entirely disclaim all belief in the idea that the Slaves of the American States are doomed to continual bodily ill-treatment. We feel convinced that the Legree-ism permeating *Uncle Tom's Cabin* is base fiction, founded on gross impossibility, and that the authoress might equally well assume that maltreatment of cattle is a national characteristic of Englishmen, from the fact of the existence of a Society for Prevention of Cruelty to Animals. Slaves in America are property, like horses, dogs, and oxen; like them, they cost money, and have work to perform. If Legree have a single negro or a drove to sell, it is his interest to bring his property to market in the best possible condition, which ill-treatment would entirely prevent. An overseer, in charge of a plantation, would not dare damage his employer's property, but would strive to make that property as cheerful, strong, and healthy as possible, so as to obtain a greater remuneration from its labour. Grant all this — and it is ridiculous to deny or question it—grant that the Slaves are better clothed and fed than any class of labourers upon earth, that their bodily comforts are more secure, and their future less uncertain, still there remains against them the terrible curse—"No right which the white man is bound to respect." "No right" to "life, liberty, or the pursuit of happiness." "No right" to husband, wife, or child. "No right" —— language fails to convey the full meaning of the awful denunciation; the rights of a whole race, annihilated by a Constitution and a Declaration, commencing with the words "All men are born free and equal!"

But, as we shall hereafter show, the action was brought before the Supreme Court for reasons affecting white men solely. Dred Scott, his wife, and children had been carried into the State of Illinois, and they, therefore, claimed their freedom, on the ground that the Constitution of that State expressly inhibited Slavery. On this plea were raised questions of the meaning of the Constitution, the powers of Congress over Territories, and the validity of the

Missouri Compromise. The first two issues were left, if not pronounced, "glorious uncertainties;" but six of the judges (five of whom were citizens of Slave States) declared the Compromise "unconstitutional," two (both from Free States) that it was "constitutional," whilst one (also from a Free State) declined pronouncing any opinion thereon.

The whole case was a get up and a swindle from beginning to end. As far as Dred Scott was concerned, there could scarcely have been found twelve citizens of Missouri State, who would not have scouted the idea that Scott, or any other negro, could possess any rights whatever. But the decision of the Supreme Court was required by the pro-Slavery party for ulterior purposes, and, therefore, the verdict, in the first instance, was for the plaintiff. When the case arrived at its intended destination, the verdict was quashed on the ground of non-jurisdiction, and (here is "the wheel within a wheel") it was declared by the highest legal authority in the land, that the Federal Constitution did not mean what it had all along been supposed to mean, that the power of Congress over its own territory was crippled and confined, and that the Missouri Compromise was unconstitutional. In other words, it was in the right of no man or body of men

whatsoever, to prevent Slavery entering any territory of the Republic; and it is against this rendering
of the Constitution that the Republicans are now
struggling. When they get into office they will
soon establish a different meaning for that instrument. In process of time they will have the
opportunity of appointing lawyers of their own
party to vacant judgeships of the Supreme Court,
and the Dred Scott judgment will be reversed.
Maybe they will become frightened at the possibility
of the Constitution being twisted into meaning anything but freedom, and forthwith insert a peg in that
instrument which shall prevent any further twisting,
in the shape of an additional clause to the Constitution. To alter or modify this document, however, requires the votes of two-thirds of both Houses
of Congress; but the future is promising, and many
years will not roll over before the Constitution of the
United States declares explicitly that the four millions of coloured men, in the Southern States, cannot,
shall not, be deprived of those rights which God has
given them, which the civilized world recognizes,
and which a tyrannical gang of some three hundred
and fifty thousand Slaveholders have most blas-
phemously deprived them of.

Six years ago, the opposition to the Slave-holding

interest took the form of simple Slavery limitation, but it has already assumed nobler proportions. Scarcely a day passes, but some Representative from the North denounces the system in Congress, dealing with the institution as a national disgrace. On the 5th of last April, Mr. Lovejoy, of Illinois, addressed the House of Representatives at Washington in the following eloquent language:—

" The question is, whether Slavery is to extend beyond its present limits? They say that is the only question over which we have not exclusive jurisdiction. Slavery is called an ' institution;' but it is no institution. Sir, it is simply a practice, as polygamy is a practice. The question now is, what are the influences and what are the elements of the practice of Slavery? The morality of Slavery has been settled long ago. The ethics of it are no longer discussed. Ages and ages ago it has been settled by the priests; and now, in gorgeousness and glory, it appears like the fresh bright glows which gather round a summer's sunset. We are told that wherever Slaveholding will pay, there it will go, precisely on the same principle that wherever robbery will pay, there robbery will go—wherever piracy will pay, there piracy will go. And wherever human flesh is cheaper than thieving, cannibalism will prevail, because it will pay. Than robbery, than piracy, than polygamy, Slaveholding is worse, more wicked, more criminal, more inglorious to man, and more abhorrent to God. Slaveholding has been justly called the ' sum of all crime.' You put every crime into the moral crucible, every wickedness perpetrated among men—put all the crime on the catalogue into the moral crucible, and then dissolve them all, and the result will be Slaveholding. It has all the violence of robbery.   I am speaking earnestly before God, and what I utter is God's truth.   It has all the violence of robbery ; it has the bloody course of piracy ; it has all the offensiveness and brutalizing lusts of polygamy, all combined and concentrated in itself, with the aggravating circumstances of each and every crime that was ever known or dreamt of.   Now, sir, the justification of Slavery is placed upon three grounds—the inferiority of the enslaved race, the fact that Slavery imparts Christianity and civilization to the Slaves, and the plea that it is guaranteed by the Constitution.   These are the three main arguments that are presented to justify Slavery in itself, and consequently it is these which are claimed to justify its expansion.   The extreme men upon this question are not the only men who have logical argument on their side.   I must be right in my position, or the extreme fire-eaters must be right.   If Slavery is right in Virginia, it must be right in Kansas.   If wrong in Kansas, it must be wrong everywhere.   Now, with reference to the first point—the inferiority of the enslaved race.   We concede, as a matter of fact, the inferiority. Does it follow from that that it is right to enslave a man simply because he is inferior to me?   Sir, this is a most abhorrent doctrine.   This gives over the weak to the mercy of the strong—the poor to the mercy of the rich. This doctrine places those who are weak in intellect in the mercy of those who are gifted.   This principle of enslaving men because of their inferiority is the most revolting that was ever presented to the world. If a man is old and weak, and bowed down with years, you strike him down. If he is idiotic, you take advantage of him—if a child, you deceive him. Why, sir, this is the doctrine of the Democrats. But it is, sir, the doctrine of devils as well. (Sensation.) According to this inhuman doctrine, the strong would enslave the weak everywhere—just as the angels might enslave men because they are superior to men—just as the archangels might enslave the inferior angels. Sir, this horrible doctrine, on the same principle, would transfer the great Jehovah himself into an infernal Juggernaut, who would enslave the world under the huge rolling wheels of his omnipotence."

This speech was received by the pro-Slavery Members with marks of fierce disapprobation. The greatest confusion ensued, and Mr. Lovejoy was in imminent peril for his personal safety: crowds of Democratic Representatives rushed upon him shaking their fists and canes in his face, until the Deputy Sergeant-at-Arms was called in to restore order. With great difficulty this was effected, and Mr. Lovejoy continued his remarks by referring to the numbers of Northern females engaged in the work of education in Southern schools, asserting that but for them the South would return to barbarism. He was again interrupted, and the following scene ensued:—

11

" Mr. Singleton, of Mississippi, said that he would not allow such insinuations upon Southern women to pass. If the Member persisted in that course of remark, he (Mr. Singleton) would hold him personally accountable.

" Mr. Lovejoy said that in the 4,000,000 of Slaves, there was not one legal husband or wife, father or child, and spoke about a Presbyterian elder down South having the Gospel whipped into him with the broadside of a hand-saw, and of a young girl in this city being whipped until the blood came out of her nostrils, and then sent to the garret to die. He had sworn to support the Constitution because he loved it, but he did not interpret it in the way Southerners did.

" Mr. Bonham, of South Carolina (Democrat) : 'You violate it.'

" Mr. Ashmore, of South Carolina (Democrat): 'And perjure yourself.'

" Mr. Singleton: ' And are a negro thief into the bargain.'

" Mr. Barksdale : ' I hold no parley with a perjured negro.' (Calling a white man ' a negro ' is the harshest term of reproach amongst Southern men.)

" Mr. Lovejoy said : ' When Daniel Webster spoke of the imposition of Austria on Hungary, he remarked that the earthquake and tornado have powers, and the thunder has power, but greater than these was the power of public opinion, and before this he proposed to arraign Austria. He (Lovejoy) proposed to hold up to the retribution of public sentiment, Slaveholding in all its atrocity and hideousness, just as gentlemen had here polygamy. Public sentiment will burn and scour out Slavery, and the proper way is by the action of the Slave States themselves. He had indorsed the Helper book because he wanted to do it. He did so without asking the gentleman from Missouri (Clark) or anybody else. You shed the blood of my brother twenty years ago (for sympathizing with the Slaves), and I am here free to speak my mind. The Republican party would spring up in Kentucky, and gentlemen now here would find themselves displaced by more moderate, and, if it were not offensive, he would add, more sensible men. He wanted to say in Charleston what he could say here.'

" Mr. Bonham: 'You had better try it.'

" Mr. Lovejoy: 'I can go to England and there discuss the question of Church and State, or any other British institution ; but if I go into the Slave States and talk against Slavery, where is my protection ? '

" Mr. Miles, of North Carolina (Democrat): ' Can you go to England and incite the labouring classes there to assassinate the Queen ? '

" Mr. Lovejoy: 'I don't desire to do that. I claim the right to discuss Slavery everywhere under the Stars and Stripes. I claim it. I demand it.'

" Mr. Bonham: ' We want you to assert it.'

" Mr. Lovejoy : ' When you call us small farmers and apply other epithets against the working people of the North, we don't harm you. If a mechanic from Pennsylvania were to go South and speak about the superiority of white labour, he would be held morally responsible. You would strip him and scourge him by the hand of a Slave, and perhaps tar and feather him.'

11—2

"Mr. Barksdale : 'The meanest negro in the South is your superior.'

"Cries of 'Order' from the Republican side.

"Mr. Lovejoy, in speaking of John Brown, said he would not curse him. He would pour no execrations upon old John Brown. He condemned what he (Brown) did. He disapproved of his act. He believed, however, that his purpose was a good one, and his motives honest and truthful. John Brown stood head and shoulders above any man here until he was strangled. Any law to enslave man was as an arrangement among pirates to distribute the spoils. By what right do you of the South get together and enact laws that I or my child shall be your Slave? Every Slave has a right to run away, in spite of your laws, and to fight himself away. Were he (Lovejoy) a Slave, and were it necessary to achieve his freedom, he would not hesitate to fill up the chasm and bridge it over with the carcasses of the slain. He loved the South.

"A voice: 'We don't love you.'

"Mr. Lovejoy : 'So it was with the Saviour. They didn't love Him. (Laughter.) Gentlemen who talked of dissolving the Union, could no more do it than they could stop the shining of the sun. Virginia, instead of clothing herself in sheep's gray, should clothe herself in sackcloth and ashes, on account of Slavery, and ought to drink the waters of bitterness.'

"Mr. Martin, of Virginia (Democrat): 'If you will come into Virginia, we will hang you higher than we did John Brown.'

"Mr. Lovejoy: 'No doubt about it.'"

Our readers will here remark the quiet and gentlemanly bearing of the Northern Representative, and the unparliamentary language of his opponents. Englishmen have done the American people gross injustice in classing them with the Slaveholders of the South. The scenes of violence which are frequently enacted in the Congress of the Union come solely from Southern men, and should not be received as a national characteristic, but as the consequence of a system which brutalizes the passions and uncivilizes the man. The Americans seen in Europe belong mostly to the Slave section of the community, and have acquired their distinctive swagger and contempt for other people through living in a confined circle surrounded by inferiors. The position arrogated by them is most amusing. They assumed the title of "gentlemen of the South," treating their fellow citizens of the North with contumely, and refusing to associate with them on terms of equality. A little scene reported by the *New York Herald*, a pro-Slavery journal, furnishes an example of this assumed social superiority. It occurred on the steps of the National Hotel at Washington, no later than April last.

"Mr. Van Wyck was standing upon the front steps of the hotel with Mr. Stuart of New York and Mr. Lovejoy of Illinois. Mr. Hindman alighted from a carriage and was passing near the three gentlemen named above to enter the hotel, when Mr. Van Wyck saluted him with a bow, and the words, 'How are you, Mr. Hindman?' The latter resented the salutation with a movement of the hand towards Mr. Van Wyck, which Mr. Stuart interpreted as an intended blow, but Mr. Hindman did not reach Mr. Van Wyck. Mr. Stuart stepped between and mildly remonstrated with Mr. Hindman, and he desisted,— remarking to Mr. Stuart that Mr. Van Wyck had made a speech in the House of Representatives insulting to every Southern gentleman, and he, Mr. Hindman, could not permit Mr. Van Wyck to speak to him. Mr. Van Wyck, not having been struck, made no resistance to Mr. Hindman."

In the speech referred to, Mr. Van Wyck had denounced the Slave system in the Southern States, and this is considered by the supporters of the Administration as more than sufficient to deprive any man of the title and privileges of a gentleman. As Europeans, for the same reason, are also banned, we cannot but smile at the assumption which requires the possession of one or more African Slaves as the qualification for respectability.

SLAVERY AND THE CHURCH.

The Slave power has laid sacrilegious hands upon everything which could minister to its advantage. Nothing has resisted its influence, and we even find

most of the clergy of the Southern States " sold to
work wickedness." Slavery, denounced as it is by
men of all religious persuasions, is there not merely
excused, but held up as the duty of every right-
thinking being, as the God-ordained means for the
conversion of the children of Ham.

From the official returns of the Seventh Census of
the United States (1850), we take the following list
of places of worship belonging to the principal
denominations in the Slave districts, and the average
number of worshippers.

CHURCHES AND CHAPELS IN THE SLAVE STATES BELONGING TO THE SIX PRINCIPAL SECTS—1850.

States.	Baptists.	Episcopal.	Independents.	Presbyterian.	R. Catholic.	Methodist.
Alabama	579	17		162	5	577
Arkansas	114	2		52	7	168
Delaware	12	21		26	3	106
Florida	56	10		16	5	87
Georgia	879	20	1	97	8	795
Kentucky	803	19		224	48	530
Louisiana	77	14		18	55	125
Maryland	45	133		56	65	479
Mississippi	385	13		143	9	454
Missouri	300	11		125	65	250
North Carolina	615	50		151	4	781
South Carolina	413	72	1	136	14	484
Tennessee	616	17		363	3	861
Texas	82	5		45	13	176
Virginia	649	173		240	17	1,025
District of Columbia	6	8		6	6	16
Total	5,661	585	2	1,860	327	6,917

NUMBER OF ATTENDANTS UPON THE ABOVE—1850.

States.	Baptists.	Episcopal.	Independents.	Presbyterian.	R. Catholic.	Methodist.
Alabama	189,980	6,920		58,805	5,200	169,025
Arkansas	18,600	350		10,731	1,600	25,745
Delaware	2,975	7,650		10,100	1,630	29,300
Florida	11,985	3,810	250	5,900	1,850	20,015
Georgia	319,293	9,325		40,596	4,250	237,218
Kentucky	291,855	7,050		99,106	24,240	167,485
Louisiana	16,660	5,210		9,510	37,780	33,180
Maryland	15,950	60,105		22,635	31,100	181,715
Mississippi	113,675	4,550		48,316	3,250	121,083
Missouri	73,525	4,500		44,820	26,402	60,944
North Carolina	201,797	15,245		63,230	1,400	221,687
South Carolina	165,805	28,940	2,000	67,765	6,030	165,740
Tennessee	195,315	7,810		135,517	1,300	249,053
Texas	10,680	1,025		8,320	6,760	33,045
Virginia	247,589	79,684		103,625	7,930	323,708
District of Columbia	3,460	6,400		5,000	7,100	10,460
Total	1,879,144	248,574	2,250	733,976	167,822	2,049,403

It will be observed from the above returns that the Methodists and Baptists have almost divided the South between them, from which it might be argued that there is some peculiar adaptability in their tenets or church government for fellowship with Slavery. But it is the former sect, more especially, which is the great Slavery church, notwithstanding that Wesley, its founder, pronounced Slaveholding " the sum of all villanies." At the last Conference of Southern Methodists, held in Baltimore at the beginning of the year, the following resolutions were unanimously adopted by the reverend gentlemen present:—

" *Resolved*,—That we sincerely deplore the agitation of the Slavery question, both in Church and State, and earnestly hope and fervently pray that this discreditable and disastrous strife may speedily cease.

" *Resolved*,—That this Conference disclaims having the least sympathy with Abolitionism. On the contrary, we are determined not to hold connection with any ecclesiastical body that makes non-slaveholding a condition of membership in the Church, and that we are opposed to any inquisition upon the motives underlying the relation of master and slave.

" *Resolved*,—That the subject of Slavery should be committed exclusively to the jurisdiction of the respective conference in which it may be found to exist.

" *Resolved*,—That no action of the General Conference

can influence us to violate our principles and practices, as indicated in the foregoing declarations ; but that we will stand by the rights and interests of our people to the last extremity.

" *Resolved*,—That our mission, as ministers of the New Testament, is to preach the Gospel of the Son of God, both to master and Slave, and to devote ourselves wholly to our appropriate work of winning souls to Christ.

" *Resolved*,—That we do solemnly remonstrate against the continual aggressive discussion of the Slavery question in the newspapers and periodicals of the Church.

" *Resolved*,—That the publishing funds and establishments of the Church are common property, held in trust by the General Conference for our common and equal use.

" *Resolved*,—That any such use of our common publishing funds, newspapers, periodicals, &c., as precludes our people from the benefits of them, while they are in no false or illegitimate relation to the Union, but are faithful to its covenants, is an abuse of trust."

The Methodist Church in the United States is directed and governed by a " General Conference," but the Southern portion of the sect has long been restless and defiant of their Northern brethren. The Conference never meets but the question of Slavery brings discord into their councils; and it could scarcely be otherwise, where one portion of the body believes " the peculiar institution " to be a duty, and the other, a crime.

The Episcopalians, Presbyterians, and Catholics in the South bear but a small proportion to the above-mentioned sects, whilst Congregationalism may scarcely be said to exist. These churches do honour to their principles by the little connection they have with Slavery, and it is from their pulpits that are heard the fiercest denunciations of the system."

All that could be done by most of the parent societies in Great Britain to induce their brethren in the Southern States of the American Union to put away this reproach from their Church, has been nobly and conscientiously performed. Mr. Spurgeon has lately poured forth his eloquence against the iniquity, and has had the honour, like a second Luther, of having a volume of his sermons publicly burnt in one of the Slave States. But we have yet to learn that the Methodist Conference in this country has taken any action on the question, except to give Slaveholding Methodism a species of approval. The reverend gentlemen who visit the United States as deputations from the Parent Society have never taken that stand which was expected of them by the Northern members, but have held out the hand of fellowship to ministers and members from the Slave States, and endeavoured to steer a middle course betwixt right and wrong.

We are well aware of the difficulty attending the discussion of such a question in a foreign country, but we are at a loss to understand how English ministers of the Gospel can reconcile it to their consciences, to give the tacit consent to Slaveholding which their unmanly silence warrants. No other body of Christians possesses an organization so capable of concentration. The Methodist Sanhedrim, or Conference, wields a power only equalled by that of the Pope and a General Council. Its ramifications extend, and its decrees are implicitly followed, throughout the civilized world; and a declaration on its part that it will no longer recognize any body excusing or defending Slavery will do more towards limiting and eventually destroying that cursed system than the action of any other Church whatever. Will the Methodists of Great Britain take that stand against the iniquity which their brethren in the Northern States of the American Union have so long expected of them, and assist in removing from their sect the reproach of being "the great Slaveholding Church?" We hope so, but we fear. The Methodist Conference and Connection are so intensely conservative that, no matter what the law may be, *provided it is law,* they will render to it implicit obedience; and so mindful are they of ren-

dering "unto Cæsar the things that are Cæsar's,"
that they fall short of giving "unto God the things
that are God's." No other body of religionists affects
a similar abstraction from politics, and it is precisely because the question of American Slavery has
become a political one that they do not interfere with
or oppose it. Not so acted and taught their founder.

THE LAST PRESIDENTIAL ELECTION.

The Republican party is sometimes accused of
being the old Whig body rechristened, though their
opponents, the Democrats, are fond of declaring that
the last Whig died with Henry Clay, and that the
party was buried with him. Certain it is that nearly
all the prominent chiefs of that once powerful organization now give the weight of their influence and
talents to the Republicans. This, however, is to be
accounted for by the fact that such former issues as
federalism, the tariff, &c., have given way to the
more important question of Slavery limitation. Many
of the Democratic leaders in the North have gone
over with them, consequent upon their party having
become entirely committed to the Slave interest.
During the past eight years, State after State in the
north has dropped from the Democratic ranks, until

there are but three of them whose governors belong to that party.

This remarkable change in public feeling first showed itself during the administration of General Pierce. There had always existed an animus against Slavery in this section of the Union, which was fanned into a fierce opposition by the Fugitive Slave Act; but it required the repeal of the Missouri Compromise and the struggle in Kansas to give consistency to the opposition.

In 1852, fourteen out of the sixteen Free States voted for the Democratic nominee for President. During the succeeding four years, the administration of General Pierce proved to the North that Democracy meant Slavery extension at all odds, and the next presidential election gave only five of those States to the Democratic candidates. The nominating Convention of the party, held at Cincinnati in the month of June, 1856, found some difficulty in selecting a canditate for the succession. General Pierce offered himself for re-election, but the party leaders knew better than to support a man politically used-up, and who had rendered himself so universally obnoxious to the North. After lengthy examination of the claims of different statesmen, they finally fixed their choice upon Mr. Buchanan, and this for two reasons: in the first place, that gentleman had been Minister at the Court of St. James's during the previous four years, and was consequently uncommitted upon the Kansas Bill and the repeal of the Missouri Compromise; and, secondly, there was some hope of his carrying his native State, more particularly as Pennsylvania had never yet seen one of her sons in the presidential chair. Appearances seemed to presage that the Free States would go against them *en masse* upon the Slavery issue; but if Mr. Buchanan could manage to carry Pennsylvania, the election might be thrown into the House of Representatives.

Very few people in this country are acquainted with the *modus operandi* of electing a President of the United States. This is effected by means of what is called the "Electoral College," a body of men equal in number to the Senators and Representatives of the United States Legislature. Each State has a vote in the College equal to its representation in Congress, *plus* its two Senators, and the Presidential electors for each State are chosen by universal suffrage, the same as any other State officers, except in South Carolina, where they are appointed by the Legislature. The following were the votes of the various States in the Electoral College at the last Presidential election:—

FREE STATES.		SLAVE STATES.	
California	4	Alabama	9
Connecticut	6	Arkansas	4
Illinois	11	Delaware	3
Indiana	13	Florida	3
Iowa	4	Georgia	10
Maine	8	Kentucky	12
Massachusetts	13	Louisiana	6
Michigan	6	Maryland	8
New Hampshire	5	Mississippi	7
New Jersey	7	Missouri	9
New York	35	North Carolina	10
Ohio	23	South Carolina	8
Pennsylvania	27	Tennessee	12
Rhode Island	4	Texas	4
Vermont	5	Virginia	15
Wisconsin	5	Total	120
Total	176		

Making in all 296 votes, a majority of which was necessary to the election of a President. Had 149 votes not been given for one candidate, the election must have been decided in the House of Representatives at Washington, in which case there is a change in the procedure. Each State has then but one vote, and it is decided for whom of the candidates that vote is to be given, by the majority of the Congressional Representatives of each State. Should Mr. Buchanan carry all the Slave States and, in

12

addition, Pennsylvania only, there was every like-
lihood of the election going to the House, as the
" American " or " Know-Nothing " candidate would
probably carry at least one Free State. Mr.
Buchanan was, however, more fortunate, obtaining
the votes of all the Slave States except one, and of
five of the Free States, amounting to 174 votes in
the Electoral College, twenty-five more than were
absolutely necessary to a choice.

It is assumed that this mode of electing the President represents the popular will, whilst at the same
time it insures his being the President of *the States,*
which is another thing to being President *of the
people of the States.* But the ratio of votes in the
Electoral College is widely different from that of
the popular vote for Presidential electors, and it is
quite possible for a President of the United States to
represent a minority of the citizens of the Republic.
Such was the case in the election of 1844, when
Mr. Polk obtained 170 votes to Mr. Clay's 105; the
former representing 1,335,834 citizens, and the latter
1,297,033, the difference being only 38,801, whilst
62,270 votes were given for a third candidate, Mr.
Birney.

In the election of 1856, Mr. Buchanan received
45 per cent. of the popular vote and 59 per cent.

of Presidential electors; Colonel Fremont, 30 per cent. of vote and 39 per cent. of electors; and Mr. Fillmore 25 per cent. of vote and only 2 per cent. of electors.

At the Presidential election to be held this year, in November next, the Electoral College will be increased to 303 votes, consequent upon the admission of Minnesota and Oregon into the Union. The former State furnishes four votes and the latter three; and any candidate must receive at least 152 votes to be elected President.

It was the running of a third candidate in the last Presidential election which caused Mr. Buchanan's success. That candidate, Mr. Millard Fillmore, was chosen Vice-President of the Republic in 1848, but the President, General Taylor, dying during his term of office, Mr. Fillmore became chief magistrate of the Confederation. The " American," or " Know-Nothing" party selected him as their candidate from reasons difficult to define. Their principles were essentially proscriptive, and though professedly aimed against all foreigners alike were mainly intended to prevent the interference of Irishmen in American politics.

The Irish had, for some years, played an important part in the politics of many States, and

12—2

they were comparatively all-powerful in some of the larger cities. Their proceedings at elections partook somewhat of the nature of riots, and generally ensured the triumph of the Democratic party. In certain wards or parishes of the cities of New York and Philadelphia, electors known to be opposed to the Democracy were maltreated by them, and prevented approaching the polls. In exchange for this support, the party gave up to them a number of municipal and county offices, and the Irish have consequently remained steadfast in their adherence, so that it is difficult to find an Irishman throughout the Union who does not glory in being a " Dimocrat." The " Know-Nothings " sought to combat this influence by preventing any foreigner having the right to vote until he had resided twenty years in the country; and, at first, they appeared to be carrying all before them. Their organization was secret, as was the meaning of the title they assumed, and this very mystery was, perhaps, the reason of their success at the outset. But the Kansas struggle gave birth to new questions, and their supporters fell away, some to join the pro-Slavery, others the Free State party.

The following professions of political faith of the three parties, will best define the issues at stake in

the election which resulted in the choice of Mr.
Buchanan :—

THE DEMOCRATIC PLATFORM.

The Democratic profession of faith is too lengthy a
document for us to quote entire, but the following are its
salient points. It was adopted at the Convention held at
Cincinnati, on the 6th of June, 1856.

The platform commences by declaring Federalism to be
injurious to the interests of the Union, and that the Federal
Government being one of limited power, it cannot carry
on a general system of internal improvements, nor become
responsible for debts contracted by any State. It declares
that the Democratic party is opposed to a National Bank,
and to taking from the President the right of veto. It
denounces the American or Know-Nothing party, and
passes to the question of Slavery, on which it ob-
serves :—

" Congress has no power under the Constitution to interfere with or control the domestic institutions of the several
States, and that all such States are the sole and proper
judges of everything appertaining to their own affairs not
prohibited by the Constitution ; that all efforts of the
Abolitionists or others, made to induce Congress to interfere with questions of Slavery, or to take incipient steps
in relation thereto, are calculated to lead to the most
alarming and dangerous consequences, and that all such
efforts have an inevitable tendency to diminish the happiness of the people and endanger the stability and perma-
nency of the Union, and ought not to be countenanced by
any friend of our political institutions."

It then goes on to declare that the Fugitive Slave Act "cannot, with fidelity to the Constitution, be repealed, or so amended as to destroy its efficiency;" and endorses the Kansas Act "as embodying the only sound and safe solution of the Slavery question."

The platform concludes with declarations upon the foreign policy of the Confederation advocating Free Seas, the Monroe Doctrine, and such measures in the West Indies, Central America, &c., as are found in the resolutions given in a former chapter. In reference to Free Trade, it declares its unalterable determination "to resist all monopolies and exclusive legislation for the benefit of the few at the expense of the many." And, finally, it endorses every act of the previous Administration.

THE AMERICAN, OR KNOW-NOTHING PLATFORM.

(*Convention held at Philadelphia, February* 22, 1856.)

Resolved, — 1. An humble acknowledgment to the Supreme Being, for his protecting care vouchsafed to our fathers in their successful revolutionary struggle, and hitherto manifested to us, their descendants, in the preservation of the liberties, the independence, and the union of these States.

2. The perpetuation of the Federal Union and Constitution, as the palladium of our civil and religious liberties, and the only sure bulwarks of American Independence.

3. *Americans must rule America,* and to this end *native*-born citizens should be selected for all State, Federal, and municipal offices of Government employment, in preference to all others. *Nevertheless,*

4. Persons born of American parents residing temporarily abroad, should be entitled to all the rights of native-born citizens.

5. No person should be selected for political station (whether of native or foreign birth) who recognizes any allegiance or obligation of any description to any foreign prince, potentate, or power, or who refuses to recognize the Federal and State Constitutions (each within its sphere) as paramount to all other laws, as rules of political action.

6. The unequalled recognition and maintenance of the reserved rights of the several States, and the cultivation of harmony and fraternal goodwill between the citizens of the several States, and to this end, non-interference by Congress with questions appertaining solely to the individual States, and non-intervention by each State with the affairs of any other State.

7. The recognition of the right of native-born and naturalized citizens of the United States, permanently residing in any territory thereof, to frame their constitution and laws, and to regulate their domestic and social affairs in their own mode, subject only to the provisions of the Federal Constitution, with the privilege of admission into the Union whenever they have the requisite population for one Representative in Congress : *Provided always*, that none but those who are citizens of the United States, under the Constitution and laws thereof, and who have a fixed residence in any such territory, ought to participate in the formation of the Constitution, or in the enactment of laws for said Territory or State.

8. An enforcement of the principles that no State or Territory ought to admit others than citizens to the right of suffrage, or of holding political offices of the United States.

9. A change in the laws of naturalization, making a continued residence of twenty-one years, of all not heretofore provided for, an indispensable requisite for citizenship hereafter, and excluding all paupers, and persons convicted of crime, from landing upon our shores ; but no interference with the vested rights of foreigners.

10. Opposition to any union between Church and State; no interference with religious faith or worship, and no test oaths for office.

11. Free and thorough investigation into any and all alleged abuses of public functionaries, and a strict economy in public expenditures.

12. The maintenance and enforcement of all laws constitutionally enacted until said laws shall be repealed, or shall be declared null and void by competent judicial authority.

13. Opposition to the reckless and unwise policy of the present Administration in the general management of our national affairs, and more especially as shown in removing " Americans " (by designation) and Conservatives in principle, from office, and placing foreigners and Ultraists in their places ; as shown in a truckling subserviency to the stronger, and an insolent and cowardly bravado towards the weaker powers; as shown in re-opening sectional agitation, by the repeal of the Missouri Compromise ; as shown in granting to unnaturalized foreigners the right of

suffrage in Kansas and Nebraska; as shown in its vacillating course on the Kansas and Nebraska question; as shown in the corruptions which pervade some of the departments of the Government; as shown in disgracing meritorious naval officers through prejudice or caprice; and as shown in the blundering mismanagement of our foreign relations.

14. Therefore, to remedy existing evils, and prevent the disastrous consequences otherwise resulting therefrom, we would build up the "American party" upon the principles hereinbefore stated.

15. That each State Council shall have authority to amend their several constitutions, so as to abolish the several degrees and substitute a pledge of honour, instead of other obligations, for fellowship and admission into the party.

16. A free and open discussion of all political principles embraced in our platform.

REPUBLICAN PLATFORM.

(Convention held at Philadelphia, June 17, 1856.)

This Convention of Delegates assembled in pursuance of a call addressed to the people of the United States, without regard to past political differences or divisions, who are opposed to the repeal of the Missouri Compromise, to the policy of the present Administration, to the extension of Slavery into Free Territory; in favour of admitting Kansas as a Free State, of restoring the action of the

Federal Government to the principles of Washington and Jefferson, and who purpose to unite in presenting candidates for the offices of President and Vice-President, do resolve as follows:—

Resolved,—That the maintenance of the principles promulgated in the Declaration of Independence, and embodied in the Federal Constitution, is essential to the preservation of our republican institutions, and that the Federal Constitution, the rights of the States, and the Union of the States, shall be preserved.

Resolved,—That with our republican fathers we hold it to be a self-evident truth, that all men are endowed with the inalienable rights to life, liberty, and the pursuit of happiness, and that the primary object and ulterior designs of our Federal Government were, to secure these rights to all persons within its exclusive jurisdiction; that, as our republican fathers, when they had abolished Slavery in all our national territory, ordained that no person should be deprived of life, liberty, or property, without due process of law, it becomes our duty to maintain this provision of the Constitution against all attempts to violate it for the purpose of establishing Slavery in any territory of the United States, by positive legislation, prohibiting its existence or extension therein. That we deny the authority of Congress, of a territorial legislature, of any individual or association of individuals, to give legal existence to Slavery in any territory of the United States, while the present Constitution shall be maintained.

Resolved,—That the Constitution confers upon Congress sovereign power over the territories of the United States

for their government, and that in the exercise of this
power it is both the right and the duty of Congress to
prohibit in the territories those twin relics of barbarism—
Polygamy and Slavery.

Resolved,—That while the Constitution of the United
States was ordained and established by the people in order
to form a more perfect Union, establish justice, ensure
domestic tranquillity, provide for the common defence, and
secure the blessings of liberty, and contains ample provisions for the protection of the life, liberty, and property
of every citizen, the dearest constitutional rights of the
people of Kansas have been fraudulently and violently
taken from them—their territory has been invaded by an
armed force—spurious and pretended legislative, judicial,
and executive officers have been set over them, by whose
usurped authority, sustained by the military power of the
Government, tyrannical and unconstitutional laws have
been enacted and enforced—the rights of the people to
keep and bear arms have been infringed—test oaths of an
extraordinary and entangling nature have been imposed,
as a condition of exercising the right of suffrage and holding office—the right of an accused person to a speedy and
public trial by an impartial jury has been denied—the
right of the people to be secure in their persons, houses,
papers and effects against unreasonable searches and
seizures has been violated—they have been deprived of
life, liberty, and property, without due process of law—
that the freedom of speech and of the press has been
abridged—the right to choose their representatives has
been made of no effect—murders, robberies, and arsons

have been instigated and encouraged, and the offenders
have been allowed to go unpunished—that all these things
have been done with the knowledge, sanction, and pro-
curement of the present Administration, and that for
this high crime against the Constitution, the Union, and
humanity, we arraign the Administration, the President,
his advisers, agents, supporters, apologists, and accessories,
either before or after the facts, before the country and
before the world, and that it is our fixed purpose to bring
the actual perpetrators of these atrocious outrages, and
their accomplices, to a sure and condign punishment
hereafter.

Resolved,—That Kansas should be immediately admitted
as a State of the Union, with her present free Constitution,
as at once the most effectual way of securing to her citizens
the enjoyment of the rights and privileges to which they
are entitled, and of ending the civil strife now raging in
her territory.

Resolved,—That the highwayman's plea, that "might
makes right," embodied in the Ostend Circular, was in
every respect unworthy of American diplomacy, and would
bring shame and dishonour upon any government or people
that gave it their sanction.

Resolved,—That a railroad to the Pacific Ocean, by the
most central and practicable route, is imperatively demanded by the interests of the whole country, and that
the Federal Government ought to render immediate and
efficient aid in its construction; and, as an auxiliary
thereto, the immediate construction of an emigrant route
on the line of railroad.

Resolved,—That appropriations by Congress for the improvement of rivers and harbours, of a national character, required for the accommodation and security of our existing commerce, are authorized by the Constitution, and justified by the obligation of Government to protect the lives and property of its citizens.

Resolved,—That we invite the affiliation and co-operation of free men of all parties, however differing from us in other respects, in support of the principles herein declared; and, believing that the spirit of our institutions, as well as the Constitution of our country, guarantee liberty of conscience and equality of rights among citizens, we oppose all legislation impairing their security.

The Presidential contest turned, mainly, upon the result of the Pennsylvania State elections held in October of the same year. It was known that as Pennsylvania went, so would go the contiguous State of New Jersey in the following month, and every exertion was made by all the parties to carry it in favour of their candidates. The Democrats were numerically superior to either of the others, but in addition to being divided upon the Slavery question, some endorsing the Kansas Act, and others opposing it, there was a possibility of a coalition of Republicans and Americans, in which case they would be outvoted. They therefore took for their rallying cry, " Buchanan and *Free* Kansas," deceiving thou-

sands of unthinking electors, who eventually discovered that Mr. Buchanan's Administration held
precisely the same policy with regard to Slavery
extension as that of General Pierce. By an admi-
rable system of tactics, they (the Democrats) carried
the State election with a few hundreds majority,
obtained in the city of Philadelphia; but this majority
was so narrow, that every effort was required to
prevent a coalition of their opponents upon one
Presidential electoral ticket. The Know-Nothing
party had split itself into two sections in the State,
one being opposed to Slavery extension, and calling
themselves "North Americans," the other upholding
the principle of "non-interference with the rights of
the South"—being, in other words, pro-Slavery men
at heart. The North Americans coalesced with the
Republicans upon the understanding, that if they
carried the twenty-seven votes of their State, each
of their candidates should have half the votes, the
twenty-seventh being given to whichever should
obtain the larger number of votes in the Electoral
College. The "Straight-out Americans" "stuck"
to their original ticket of twenty-seven Fillmore
electors, thus playing into the hands of the Democracy, and, as many thought, intentionally so. The
result was, Mr. Buchanan carried the State by

83,200 over Fremont, the Republican candidate, and by 148,535 over Fillmore, his entire majority being only 626—an exceedingly narrow one in 460,395, the number polled for the three candidates.

Four other Free States, California, Illinois, Indiana, and New Jersey, also went for Mr. Buchanan, giving him, with the fourteen Slave States, 174 votes in the Electoral College—twenty-five votes more than were absolutely necessary to elect him President. Mr. Fillmore carried only one State, Maryland.

Had the Republicans and Americans in Pennsylvania agreed upon a single electoral ticket as early as the beginning of September, and subsequently agitated the State together, they would have carried the October elections against the Democracy, and defeated Mr. Buchanan in November. The choice of President would then have fallen upon the House of Representatives at Washington, for no candidate would have received the necessary number of votes in the Electoral College.

MR. BUCHANAN'S ADMINISTRATION.

Mr. Buchanan was not long in office before his administration had alienated the Northern supporters of the party. One of his first measures was the lowering of the tariff. It may be well to observe that the producing States in the South are Free Trade, whilst the manufacturing North is inclined towards Protection. It will have been remarked, in the declaration of principles of the Democratic party, that Free Trade principles are emphatically asserted, implying that other parties were opposed to them.

The iron interest of Pennsylvania deeply resented this reduction in the Customs Duties; this, added to the pro-Slavery character of the new Government, soon told upon the State, and the Republican party have carried it in the last two elections. Of all the Northern or Free States, California alone continues faithful to the Democracy.

The late election of a Republican Speaker in the House of Representatives was a serious blow to the pro-Slavery party, followed up by the selection of Mr. Forney to the Clerkship of the House. It is to this gentleman Mr. Buchanan was mainly indebted for his nomination at the Cincinnati Convention, and his eventual success in Pennsylvania. Mr. Forney is immensely powerful in that State, and the whole of his influence there and elsewhere is now given against his former client and party. The night after his election as Clerk, Mr. Forney addressed a public meeting at Washington, and as the speech he then

delivered portrays the state of feeling amongst Mr.
Buchanan's former supporters in the North, we shall
proceed to give it entire, as reported.   It is as
follows:—

" Citizens of Washington,—I have a few words to say to
you upon the event of this day.   I desire to address them
to those inside as well as those outside, in deference to
what has transpired in the House of Representatives
to-day.   For this sentiment, demonstrated in my own
person, I am most sincerely thankful to you, and I regard
it as a testimony of approval of the result of the day's
proceedings.   I say, gentlemen, there is something peculiar
in this demonstration; and first, let me say, peculiar to
myself.   Gentlemen, four years ago this very evening the
House of Representatives of the United States, after a long
and most harassing session, was at last organized by the
election of Nathaniel P. Banks, of Massachusetts, as
Speaker.   In the discharge of the duties of Clerk of that
body, the same as performed by Mr. Allen, who retires
to-day, I had the honour to receive, at the hands of the
representatives of the people, a unanimous endorsement
for the manner in which I had discharged the duties of
the Clerk of Congress, which I then held.   Now, gentlemen, just four years have elapsed to-day since my retire-
ment from that office, when now, by the expression of the
representatives of my own region, I am again returned to
the same position from which I then voluntarily retired,
clothed with the confidence of the whole people of the
United States.   In these four years, gentlemen, many

13

changes have taken place. I retired from the Clerk's chair in the year 1856, with my heart ardently beating to see the man whom I then conceived to be the favourite son of Pennsylvania elected to the Presidential chair. Gentlemen, I had had no hope in life before that—no aim or object. Then all was concentrated in the one absorbing feeling to see that man's aspirations carried out to a successful issue. I assisted in his triumph. I came back to the State where I was born, and then, with whatever selfishness was in me, if any, I gave it all to that man and to his cause; and the result was, that he was elected President of the United States—to the high office of presiding for a time over the destinies of this great country. We, in our part of the country, believe, gentlemen, that the district of Columbia is common ground—that it is mine as it is your home. I believe, and I know that I have a right to speak here, as I have a right to speak in Philadelphia, at least that there is no ostracism and no proscription of sentiment or freedom of speech tolerated. When that is proscribed, when free men, from whatever State of the Union they may come, are denied freedom of speech, then your Union is virtually dissolved. And therefore it is that in this place and in this presence I desire to say, that in electing James Buchanan we thought we acted in accordance with the spirit of Democratic institutions, Slavery inclusive. That had been written in the bond. Heretofore for some time there had been no going back of the bond, but after his (Mr. Buchanan's) election, when his elevation to the chair of office was secured, he disregarded his pledges, and it was discovered that a new reading had been suggested, a new gospel presented to our faith, and thus we who at first acted with him, never believing that we who had adhered to his faith should be excluded from the Democratic party, concluded to stand by it. Consequently, the result has been as you foresaw. That result is, that the General Government of the country has turned all its power against the men standing in my relation to it, and James Buchanan, elevated to be President of the United States, has become a despot—a despot more intolerant than any ever before known in the history of this country, and has performed acts of tyranny which, if attempted in despotic France, would create a revolution. I say it with pain for Philadelphia, that never in the history of the country, never in the annals of any President, has there been such a proscription of men—never such a proscription of individual opinions. When he was raised to that high position which he has disgraced, raised by the votes of the people of the North, he pledged himself upon bended knees to sustain the true policy of the country. But now what do I see? Why, I see him turning against his own people, and crouching once more upon his knees, this time before the South, that despises him for his cowardice.

" When I see all this, and when I see, also, that the great Democratic party have not risen in arms to protest against it, I have only to say for myself that I for one will not submit to it. I will not, I say, submit to it, but I will join hands with any party—with Americans, with Republicans, with any party of men—to rebuke such proscription as this is. If you tell me from this that therefore I

13—2

am opposed to the institutions of the South, I say no.
And I reply, that, on the contrary, I feel the same devotion to the South that I have ever felt.   Now, let me say,
without protracting these desultory remarks, let me say
with regard to the Republican members, that they have
been most atrociously slandered, that the whole Republican
party of the North have been slandered, in having been
held responsible for the unfortunate outrage at Harper's
Ferry.   There have been expressions, and opinions, and
sentiments uttered against the leaders of the Republican
party against which all honest instinct, and even party
prejudices revolt.   What is the actual truth?   Why, the
very moment that the news of that invasion reached the
North they were struck with horror, and there was not a
man who did not denounce and who did not deplore it.
We have in these days some singular statesmen, particularly among those who are allied to the Administration
party, and amongst them there are some who aspire to be
candidates for the Presidency.   But I say this business of
holding a whole party responsible for the acts of a few
individuals has gone out of fashion.   What I ask is, are
the Democratic party of the North, who have supported
the rights of the adopted citizens of the country, to be held
responsible for the votes of those representatives in Congress
here who voted for acts inimical to the rights and privileges of the country's adopted children?   Certainly not.
Hence I protest against the assumption that the people of
my region are in favour or would support any set of men
who approve of the doctrines of the Helper book, or who
put themselves forward as the champions of those who

would attempt to invade the State of Virginia, and crimson her soil with the blood of her people. But we are told that while all other men are to be forgiven for their peculiar doctrines, that while the American party are to be forgiven, the Republican party are to receive no absolution. If you allow me to say—but I think I will say it whether you allow me to or not—the Democratic party, to which Mr. Buchanan has bound himself, is devoted solely to the perpetuation and extension of Slavery. But I, as one man who is resolved to stand by the rights of the South, who is resolved to see the Fugitive Slave Law executed in the letter and the spirit, who is resolved to march forward if necessary as a humble man in arms—I am resolved for one to protest against such an act. This country has a higher, a nobler, and loftier destiny before it than the extension or perpetuation of Slavery. I say it frankly, that I regret that it is in existence. I speak as I feel, and when I see all the power of this Government exercised for the protection and perpetuation of that institution, I must protest against it.

"I have seen for the last eight weeks men, Northern men —and I was ashamed to see them—lending themselves to the depravity—if I may be permitted to use the term, but certainly to the degradation—of endorsing principles never before witnessed. But, gentlemen, to bring, as I said before, these desultory remarks to a close, let me, in conclusion, repeat my thanks for this demonstration. You may remember this passage in *Mazeppa*—my friend, Mr. Jackson, of Kentucky, will also remember—when Mazeppa (I cannot repeat the exact words) is bound to a wild steed,

which is turned off, and which flew with him over moun-
tains, through valleys and forests, and across rivers, pur-
sued by wolves, shouts back to his tyrant and persecutor,
that some day he would return to repay him. 'Some
day I will return,' said Mazeppa, 'to thank you, Count,
for this uncourteous ride.'   Gentlemen, I have had the
ride for the last two or three years, but I have also,
Mazeppa-like, come back to settle with the respectable
and venerable gentleman at the other end of the avenue
for that ride.   I am returned to pay him my respects.   I
have returned to settle accounts with him.   If he is now
sitting in his easy chair at home to-night he must hear
your loud and hearty cheers, and they will remind him
that his old friend Forney has come back to settle the old
debt with him."

However much we may esteem the motives which
prompted John Brown in his attempted raising of
the Slaves in Virginia, it is impossible to defend his
action upon any grounds whatever.   John Brown
was not a citizen of Virginia, and, in invading that
State, he broke every law, human and divine.   In
our admiration for his courage and disinterestedness,
coupled with our detestation of Slavery, we have
overlooked the fact that the " peculiar institution "
of the South is guaranteed from outside interference
by the Federal Constitution, and that it can only be
abrogated by the action of the State in which it

exists. Brown was an honest but misguided fanatic, and should receive no more consideration from Englishmen, than we accorded to Smith O'Brien and his fellow conspirators, whilst his success would have led to infinitely more disastrous consequences. Brown's true arena was in acting with the Republicans, who propose to stay the further spread of Slavery, *and by constitutional and righteous means* to finally destroy it.

It is a new phase in American politics that such sentiments as those of Mr. Forney can be declared openly at Washington. The Senate House itself did not formerly protect a man who bearded the Slave interest; and it is comparatively fresh in the recollection of all how the Hon. Charles Sumner came near losing his life for daring to use certainly not stronger language. But the times and public opinion have changed since then, and Mr. Forney is too influential a personage to meddle with. He is the most skilful organizer in the Democracy, knowing better than any else how to work the electors; and, in losing him, the Democracy have lost the States of Pennsylvania and New Jersey, representing thirty-four votes in the Electoral College.

As these two States, so have Indiana and Illinois declared for freedom, and when it is considered that

the elections of any State preceding the Presidential
contest foretell for which party the State will then
vote, the hopes of the Democracy may well be
crushed. At the present hour the Republicans are
not merely the majority of the North, but the North
itself; and we can appreciate the rage which the
Slave power must feel in the reins of government
being torn from its hands. In the days of the old
Whig party the spirit of rivalry carried Federalists
and Democrats to no greater lengths than in English
elections of the olden time; for whichever might be
successful, there was little fear of " the peculiar institution " suffering. Now, however, resort is had to
personal violence, and threats of civil war and separation from the Free States are made not merely by
private individuals, but by Governors and Senators of
the South. One of the foremost of these "fire-
eaters," as they are well termed in American political
phraseology, is the late Governor of Virginia, Mr.
Wise, a gentleman who is regarded in the light of
a representative Southerner. In a speech delivered
by him at a public meeting a few weeks back he
thus expresses himself: —

" I am assailed, because I am too much of a Union man
—so much so that I am for '*fighting in the Union*.' I believe I never used that expression before, but I will adopt

it now. And I ask, who will not fight in the Union, and
out of the Union, both, if necessary, rather than be deprived of his essential rights, and be dishonoured, degraded,
and oppressed? The man, I say, who will not first fight
in the Union, will never fight out of it. I went to fight
John Brown and his aiders and abettors *in the Union, and
would have marched through the Union to Canada, to over-
take and subdue any lawless men, invaders of the Constitution and the Union or any soil of the Union.*"

*   *   *   *   *

" And when compelled to fight, whether they (the Republicans) or I will be guilty of treason, will depend upon
the right and the law of the case, and the success of the
conflict will be and shall be determined by arms. If they
assail me, and I conquer them in the fight, and I have the
Constitution and the law on my side, I will hang them as
we did John Brown, and Cooke and Coppie."

One would suppose that ex-Governor Wise and
his section of the country were preparing to defend
themselves from the assaults of some powerful op-
pressor. But all this gasconade means nothing more
than that the Southern States are resolved to maintain their asserted right to breed and carry Slaves
where they choose. He therefore explains the ob-
jects of himself and party :—

" As for me, I will have the Union and the negroes
both ! That is my position. And if I cannot maintain it

otherwise, I will have revolution ; and the end of that revolution shall be to defend the Constitution and restore the Union.

"If the last extremity must come—if separation must take place—I am for preparing first to take the *de facto* and *de jure* powers of the Confederacy into our own hands, and not for leaving them in the hands of enemies who would endeavour to hang me for treason."

Mr. Wise proposes, in the event of the Northern States electing the next President, to march upon Washington, and seize the reins of government before the new President has time to take his seat. He is well aware that this would lead to an open rupture with the North, but declares his conviction that war will prevent a dissolution of the Union. He says,—

"The truth is—and the sooner it is realized and admitted the better—you cannot separate the States of this Union without conflict, without a civil war over the division which may be claimed. Whenever either party resolves upon a separation, that party must be prepared for intestine war.

"And, sirs, I tell you, that if, as brave and faithful men, we show ourselves indeed ready and earnest in the intent to strike the actual blow of armed resistance against aggression, the aggression itself will be withdrawn and atoned for before the blow can possibly be stricken. Once convince the black Republicans and Abolitionists of the North that you will fight, and fight at once, for the maintenance of your rights, and they will not only abstain from further aggression, but you will promptly drive them back to the walls of the Constitution and the muniments of the Union. Instead of stirring up intestine war, as some gentlemen so tremulously predict, you will put an end to all apprehension of strife, and especially to that war of sectional hatred and malice which is now raging against you with a virulence and continually increasing disaster worse than any calamity which could result from a just and rightful appeal to the God of battles.

" It is with the Union of the States of my country as it is with the union of matrimony. It is holy and sacred in its plighted faith, and its obligations are assumed for better or for worse, in sickness and in health, and they are perpetual. The husband of such an union is bound to bear and forbear much and long, and to the uttermost—until the point of honour is touched. But the moment his honour is touched, he is bound to burst the bonds of union like burning withes from around him. When that is touched, the union must be dissolved at all hazards, or it becomes a degrading domination not to be endured, except by the abjectly debased. The sole question to be settled, then, is whether the wrong-doer or the wronged party shall be driven from the marital possessions by the divorce? Feeling that I am not the assailant, but the assailed—not the wrong-doer, but the wronged—when my honour is touched I will drive the assailant and the wrong-doer from the bed and board of the Union, and I will not consent to yield it to any who have prostituted its powers and blasted my peace. If black Republican outrage obliges the dissolution of the Union, then let the Abolitionists go—let them be driven to Canada, or to utter destruction, or further, if they can. I would reserve for my State and for my section, wronged as they have been and they still are, all the powers and possessions of the Union."

Mr. Wise stands in the front rank of Southern statesmen, and the above speech furnishes an index to the state of feeling in the Slave districts. His successor in the gubernatorial office, Governor Letcher, recommends a similar policy in his annual message to the Virginia Legislature delivered on the 7th of last January. He complains that the Northern States have interfered with the rights of the South, and that many of the Legislatures have passed laws which render inoperative the Fugitive Slave Act. The Governor expresses his belief that the North has, of late years, put a totally different construction upon the Federal Constitution than the South can permit, and suggests that a Convention of all the States be summoned to ascertain whether these differences cannot be settled without resort to extremities. If the Free States refuse to meet in Convention for such purpose, or, after meeting, decline the construction offered by the South, it will furnish reason for severing the Union. He also suggests that a commission of two of the most experienced Virginian statesmen be sent to the different Northern Legislatures, for the purpose of demanding a repeal of the Acts which obstruct the operation of the Fugitive Slave Law, and he finally recommends a revision of the Militia code, the procuring of muni- tions of war, and the organizing of brigades of minute men.

Most of the other Slave States have taken a similar position in reference to the present aspect of affairs; but the free North is not to be turned from its purpose by such menaces. The struggle in Kansas proved that Republicans could carry their point over any amount of opposition, and their success in the event of Civil War, will certainly be enhanced by having the forces and treasury of the Confederation at their disposal. If the Southern States be united in one common object, their opponents are equally so, and should the majority of the Union return a free- soil successor to Mr. Buchanan next November, the North will be unanimous and determined in his support.

Mr. Buchanan's administration has succeeded in breaking up the Democratic party in the Free States. The demoralization has extended even to the Catholic

Irish, and the very leaders who still act with the Democracy are preparing to join the Republicans. One of the most able and influential supporters of the party, Mr. Bronson, of the New York *Quarterly Review,* has lately animadverted in strong terms upon the general policy of the present Administration. We make a lengthy extract, not merely to prove the extent of the stampede from the Democratic ranks, but because the writer gives a clear insight into the general government of the Confederation, during the past four years. Mr. Bronson says:—

" We can hardly call to mind a single statesmanlike measure that he (Mr. Buchanan) has recommended, nor a wise act of much magnitude his Administration has performed. If he has defended a sound constitutional principle, he has coupled its defence with a principle or measure of a totally different character. In the Kansas affair his course is indefensible; for, though right in maintaining that it is not necessary to the validity of the constitution that it be submitted to the people for ratification, he was wrong in promising the people of Kansas that it should be so submitted; and equally wrong in accepting and presenting the Lecompton Constitution to Congress as the constitution of the State of Kansas, knowing as he did that the Lecompton Convention and its Constitution were a manifest fraud.

*   *   *   *   *

" In his foreign politics, the President seems not to have

been wise, active, or successful. He might easily, when minister to Great Britain, if he had been so disposed, have settled satisfactorily the Central American question, but he preferred to leave it open as an issue to help his nomination and election to the Presidency, and as a chance to acquire glory to his Administration. Its settlement seems now further off than ever, and has by mismanagement become so complicated that, if ever settled, it will receive a Franco-British, not an American solution. For ourselves, we shall be glad to see it settled in any way that will secure a free transit across the Isthmus to the commerce of all nations, and close the Central American States to the operations of filibusters.

"We have, no doubt, just causes of complaint against Mexico, a republic which can hardly be regarded as a State; but the lust for territorial acquisition has prevented our Government from either taking the proper steps to obtain justice for our own citizens, or offering its own friendly offices to assist the distracted republic in re-establishing legal order and preserving peace. We have been quite willing to see her fall to pieces, counting with certainty on getting the fragments at our convenience. We have thought that a little idle declamation about the ' Monroe doctrine,' wholly inapplicable to the case, would guard our destined prey from any attempt on the part of an European power to snatch it from us ; but without an army, and with a navy inferior to that of Spain, our fulminations of the Monroe doctrine are not remarkably terrifying to Europeans, and we find now that France and England are quite likely to disregard them.

The proposition of the President to Congress, to authorize him to invade and establish a protectorate over the northern provinces of the Republic, has aroused the vigilance and activity of Great Britain, and we shall, hereafter, have to reckon with her in Mexico as well as in Nicaragua and Costa Rica.   *   *   *   *   *

" A war with Great Britain is out of the question. Our mercantile classes, our cotton and rice planters, our pork, beef, and wheat growers would shrink from it with horror. She is the great consumer of our raw products, and the centre of our exchanges with whatever part of the world we trade.

" We should have no serious objection to see Cuba one of the States of this Union, and it is a 'fixed idea' of the American people, that, if she passes from the possession of Spain, she must pass into that of no other power. That she may, some day, be annexed to the Union, is far from improbable; but the Bill introduced into the Senate, at the recommendation of the President, appropriating thirty millions of dollars towards obtaining it by purchase, is one of the coolest things we have read of in history, and we know not whether to regard it as the more insulting to our national honour or to Spain.

" It is true, we purchased of Napoleon I. the territory of Louisiana, and purchased it at a bargain ; but it was in the market, and if there was dishonour, it was on the part of the Sovereign who offered it for sale, not on the part of the State that saw fit to purchase it. But Cuba is not in the market, and the President is as well aware of that fact as we are.   *   *   *   *   *

" There is something even more insulting in the reasons which it is proposed to offer to Spain to induce her to sell Cuba, than even the proposition itself to buy it. Our minister is to say to the Spanish Government : " Your possession of Cuba is distant and precarious, and it costs you a large sum annually to defend it, an expense which, in your present straitened circumstances, you can ill afford. We want Cuba; it is indeed very important, almost necessary, to us, and we are ready and willing to buy it at a very liberal price, and hand you over the price for it. You had better close with us at once, for if you will not sell it to us, we shall be obliged in our own interest to take it, and you will lose it and get nothing." We forget that it is precisely we who render her possession of Cuba precarious, and our disloyal acts that render necessary the enormous expenditures for its preservation to the Spanish Crown ; that the series of acts that render its possession precarious are ours, and that these acts on our part are done precisely in order to force her to sell it. . . . . But nobody is deceived in the case. Neither the President, nor Congress, neither Benjamin * the Jew, nor Bennett † the Scotsman, expects to obtain Cuba by

* Senator Benjamin of Louisiana, who introduced the Bill into Congress.

† James Gordon Bennett, Editor of the *New York Herald*,— Mr. Buchanan's organ in the north. Mr. Bennett emigrated from Scotland when young, and started the above paper, which, for many years, has held a foremost place in the American press. He constantly supported the pro-Slavery democracy until the presidency of General Pierce, whom he greatly assisted in electing, but subsequently opposed with extreme violence. Professedly advocating the election of Colonel Fremont, in 1856, he rendered

14

purchase. The offer to buy and pay is intended after the act is done, to be a plea in justification to public opinion for taking possession of the island by force or revolution. We are informed, on what ought to be very high authority in the case, that a republican insurrection is completely organized throughout the island of Cuba, so complete and strong that it is sure of success, if its leaders can only have an assurance from our Government that when they have struck the blow, declared their independence of Spain, and instituted the Republic, they will be received into the Union, as a State. . . . . The Bill has been introduced into Congress chiefly for the purpose of committing Congress and the people of the United States to the Cuban revolutionists. . . . . In a commercial point of view, it (Cuba) would perhaps extend our trade, but add little to the revenues of the Government. *It is wanted only to give us another Slave State, and to strengthen the institution of Slavery,* which after all it would weaken. The South is strong, if she remains as she is, and does not attempt to extend Slavery beyond its present limits, or to acquire new Slave Territory. Slavery and the free labour system are decidedly antagonistical, and the expansion of the one necessarily resists that of the other. It is not possible that the Slave system of labour should triumph in this country, and the South may as well give up the hope of it at once. There is yet power enough in the Southern

that election impossible by persistently opposing the union of the Republicans and Americans in doubtful States. But though advocating Democratic principles, he is both feared and hated by the party leaders, more especially in the South, for scarcely one of them has escaped unmeasured vituperation in his journal.

States, and loyalty enough to the Constitution in the Northern, to protect Slavery where it is; but let the South attempt to extend it beyond its present constitutional limits, and she will lose what she has. The attempt to go beyond the Constitution in support of Slavery, made by the Supreme Court in the Dred Scott case, has destroyed much of the respect hitherto entertained for its members, and weakened the hold of the judiciary on the public mind; and the attempt on the part of the President and advisers has demoralized the Democratic party throughout the Union. . . . . If Mr. Buchanan had taken the advice we gave him in January, 1856, he would have found himself to-day at the head of a strong Union and Constitutional party, able to elect his successor, and to govern the nation. He did not see proper to listen to it, and he finds himself now without a party, with scarcely a supporter but the *New York Herald*, and failing in almost every measure of foreign or domestic policy he has recommended. Never have our politics stood lower, never the reputation of our Republic so low."

These are the sentiments of a man still acting with the Democratic party, and who would scarcely be inclined to represent matters in a worse light than they really are.

THE NOMINATIONS FOR THE PRESIDENCY.

The nominating Convention of the pro-Slavery, Democratic party, held at Charleston, South Caro-

lina, in the month of April, found it impossible to
agree upon a candidate. The first steps in the proceedings were inharmonious, consequent upon the
demoralization of the Democracy in the North, for
the delegates could not even resolve upon a common
declaration of principles.

The Cincinnati platform of 1856* had been pur-
posely framed to read two ways, meaning one thing
in the North, and the opposite in the South. This
fact was distinctly owned to at Charleston, Southern
delegates accusing their Free State brethren of
having proposed and carried that policy; and declaring
that false impressions should no longer exist as to
the ultimate aim of their party. However honest
this resolve may appear, honesty had little influence
in the decision. If a similar "platform" could ensure
success this year, it would infallibly have been
adopted; but Mr. Buchanan's Administration had
unmasked their policy and satisfied the Northern
States of their irrevocable committal to Slavery.
They followed the only course left open to them—
an honest one, it is true, but forcedly so—a course
frequently followed by criminals brought to bay,
namely, effrontery and menace.

The majority of the "Committee on the platform"

* See page 181.

submitted a string of resolutions to the Convention, which are, beyond parallel, tyrannical. The report was endorsed by eighteen members of the Committee, three only being from Free States. The minority presented counter propositions, moving the adoption of the Cincinnati platform, but referring the question of Slavery to the Supreme Court.

The report of the majority was as follows :—

" *Resolved*,—That the platform adopted at Cincinnati be affirmed, with the following resolutions :—' That the national democracy of the United States hold these cardinal principles on the subject of Slavery in the territories :—First. That Congress has no power to abolish Slavery in the territories. Second. That the territorial Legislature has no power to abolish Slavery in the territories, nor to prohibit the introduction of Slaves therein, nor any power to destroy or impair the right of property in Slaves by any legislation whatever.

" *Resolved*,—That it is the duty of the Federal Government to protect, when necessary, the rights of persons or property on the high seas, in the territories, or wherever else its constitutional jurisdiction enters.

" *Resolved*,—That the enactments of State Legislatures to defeat the faithful execution of the Fugitive Slave Law are hostile in character, subversive of the Constitution, and revolutionary in their character.

" *Resolved*,—That it is the duty of the Government of the United States to acquire Cuba at the earliest practicable moment.

" *Resolved*,—That it is the duty of the Government of the United States to offer protection to naturalized citizens from foreign countries."

The report of the minority of the committee was adopted by the Convention by a majority of *one*, the vote being sectional ; North and South ranging themselves in opposite camps.

It will be well to note distinctly the divergence of the two sections of the Democracy upon the Slavery issue. The Southern States maintain that *property in man is before and above the Constitution* and all Federal enactments; whereas the Northern leave it a comparatively open question, subject to judicial decision. The former constitute it an *inherent right ;* the latter regard it as a *municipal ordinance* alone. They, in fact, endorse the doctrine of " squatter sovereignty," leaving the existence or non-existence of Slavery to the citizens of the States and Territories.

Upon this platform they endeavoured to elect a candidate for the Presidency in the person of Judge Douglas, United States Senator from Illinois—the author of the said doctrine of " squatter sovereignty," and father of the Nebraska-Kansas Act. The ballots cast in favour of that gentleman were insufficient to constitute him the candidate of the party : the Southern delegates seceded from the Convention, and the assembly adjourned, to meet again two months subsequently, at Richmond, in Virginia.

It is almost impossible that the Democracy can agree upon any candidate who shall represent the two opposing platforms of their party. They will, in consequence, have two candidates in the field: Judge Douglas, appealing to Northern suffrages; and a Southern statesman (probably Senator Jefferson Davis, of Mississippi), who will carry the Slave States, and endeavour to form a Southern Republic.

The American, or Know-Nothing party, proposing no solution of the difficulty now distracting the Union—representing merely the proscription of foreign-born citizens, and a desire to obtain office— have selected candidates for the Presidency and Vice-Presidency of the Republic, in the persons of Mr. Bell, of Tennessee, and the Hon. Edward Everett, the first of American orators. It is doubtful whether they will carry even one State, so overpowering is the agitation upon the Slavery issue; nor will any action of their party affect the final result.

The Republican Convention, held at Chicago in the month of May, completed its labours after a short session of three days. Their platform is merely a re-adoption and re-emphasizing of that of 1856. (See page 185.) There was some little difficulty in deciding upon their candidates, owing to an *embarras de richesses,* so many prominent statesmen being supported by the various State delegations; but, after the third ballot, Mr. Abram Lincoln, of Illinois, and Senator Hamlin, of Maine, were declared the nominees of the Free State party for the Presidency and Vice-Presidency.

It was at first supposed that Senator Seward, of New York, would be the choice of the Convention. Mr. Seward has long been recognized as the mouthpiece of the Republicans in the United States Senate; but his friends were rather the chiefs of the party than the party itself. The real cause of his non-selection lay in the fact that he was looked upon as " too conservative," and deficient in the " backbone," or determination to resist the secessionist efforts of the South.

Mr. Abram Lincoln, whom we feel justified in regarding as *the first anti-Slavery President of the United States,* is the most popular man in Illinois,— Judge Douglas's own State. All the States of the north-west — Illinois, Indiana, Iowa, Michigan, Minnesota, and Wisconsin—will vote for him, and against such an antagonist it is more than probable that Judge Douglas will refuse any nomination from the Democracy. The same must be said of Senator Hamlin, who, like Fremont in 1856, will carry Maine, Massachusetts, Connecticut, Rhode Island, New Hampshire, and Vermont.

No two candidates, whom the Republicans could select, are less "conservative" with regard to Slavery extension than these two gentlemen. Mr. Hamlin is accused by the Southern party of being "a rabid abolitionist." Mr. Lincoln's policy upon the issues at stake is well-defined, clear, and comprehensible. In February last he delivered an address in New York city upon the present aspect of political affairs, commencing his discourse as follows :—

"In his speech last autumn, at Columbus, Ohio, as reported in the *New York Times*, Senator Douglas says:

" 'Our fathers when they framed the Government under which we live, understood this question just as well and even better than we do now.'

"I fully indorse this, and I adopt it as a text for this discourse. I so adopt it because it furnishes a precise and an agreed starting point for a discussion between Republicans and that wing of the Democracy headed by Senator Douglas. It simply leaves the inquiry: 'What was the understanding those fathers had of the question mentioned?' What is the frame of Government under which we live ? The answer must be, 'The Constitution of the United States.' That Constitution consists of the original, framed in 1787 (and under which the present Government first went into operation), and twelve subsequently framed amendments, the first ten of which were framed in 1789.

"Who were our fathers that framed the Constitution? I suppose the 'thirty-nine' who signed the original instrument may be fairly called our fathers who framed that part of the present Government.

"What is the question which, according to the text, those fathers understood just as well, and even better than we do now? It is this: 'Does the proper division of local from federal authority, or anything in the Constitution, forbid our Federal Government to control as to Slavery in our federal territories? Upon this, Douglas holds the affirmative, and Republicans the negative. This affirmative and denial form an issue, and this issue—this question—is precisely what the text declares our fathers understood better than we."

Mr. Lincoln then proved, incontestably, that the fathers of the Republic frequently endeavoured to limit and confine " the peculiar institution," and that they expressly reserved to Congress all power over the territories of the Confederation.

Late advices from the United States inform us that the election of Messrs. Lincoln and Hamlin is looked upon as " a foregone conclusion " by the Administration at Washington, and the pro-Slavery leaders. Should the contest be transferred to the House of Representatives, the result is equally certain; for the majority of the delegation from nearly all the Northern States is Republican.

THE RESULT OF THE FORTHCOMING PRESIDENTIAL ELECTION.

The result of the contest next November will be the election of an anti-Slavery extension President and the annihilation of Southern terrorism. It will be the repeal of the Fugitive Slave Act, the confining of Slavery within its present limits, and the destruction of Filibusterism, Annexationizing, and the secret carrying-on of the Slave-trade.

Such *must* be the result of the Republican Party's electing its candidate to the Presidency. That it will elect him, we have merely to examine the votes in the Electoral College. The Free States possess 183 votes in that body, to 120 of the Slave section, and the Democracy can only succeed by carrying some of the former. The States they might endeavour to carry are California, Illinois, Indiana, New Jersey, Pennsylvania, Minnesota, and Oregon; representing *seriatim* the following votes:—4, 11, 13, 7, 27, 4, 3. The Democracy are pretty sure of California, for that State is entirely removed from agitation on the Slave question; but in Oregon, they may not be so successful. Illinois and Indiana are now certain to vote for the Republican candidate; whilst in Pennsylvania and New Jersey, as in Illinois and Indiana, the Republicans have carried the elections for a year or two past. Some weeks ago, the Democratic candidate for Mayor of Philadelphia was defeated; and this is a certain presage of how the State will vote in November. As Pennsylvania votes, so will New Jersey; while Minnesota will act with other Western States, all of which are thoroughly opposed to the Slave oligarchy.

Giving the pro-Slavery party the benefit of what, until the nomination of Mr. Lincoln, were regarded as "doubtful" States—namely, California, Illinois, Indiana, and Oregon; that is to say, of 31 votes—their opponents will still have the majority sufficient to elect their candidate. But California alone is *likely* to act with them; the chances are enormously in favour of the three latter going with the Republicans, inasmuch as that party has carried late elections in them by constantly increasing majorities.

The Southern States forebode the result and are avowedly preparing to resist. Will their resistance take the form of sullen discontent, or of open opposition to the Federal Government and to the Northern

States, so much their superiors in wealth, population, and intelligence?

The policy of the Slave States with regard to the general Government is represented by three parties: Unionists, Disunionists, and Nullifiers. The day has gone by for nullification. In the days of Calhoun, its apostle, it was treason to the Constitution; but nullification has become *too conservative* for the South, and the pro-Slavery leaders are, almost to a man, declaring for secession. Is there sufficient patriotism and common sense amongst the inhabitants of that section, who do not make politics a trade, to prevent the disunionist cabal carrying their plot into effect? We trust so, but " the wish is father to the thought." The Legislatures of the Slave States are more or less disunionists, and the Executives belong to the same category. Legislatures and Executives are elected by the people, and we can only infer that the people who elected them advocate the same principles.

The North will not hesitate a moment. Hundreds of thousands of bayonets will be poured into Virginia, Georgia, and the Carolinas; wherever, in fact, rebellion rears its head. To question the result would be to doubt in God and civilization.

HOW THE RESULT WILL AFFECT ENGLAND.

The immediate consequence of Southern attempts at secession will be diminution, if not cessation, of the American cotton supply.   Can we obtain sufficient of that staple from India, Natal, and other districts? Is it not high time that we endeavour to turn our West Indian and other colonies to proper account, suited as many of them are for the cultivation of cotton?   The mountainous and hilly lands of Jamaica are especially deserving of the attention of our Government, and the moment is ripe for commencing the experiment.

The Southern States of the American Union are following the example of the infatuated Louis the Fourteenth of France.   As he drove into exile thousands of his subjects engaged in manufactures and trade, who sought refuge in England and laid the foundation of our manufacturing supremacy, so are the Slave States now driving from their confines thousands of freed coloured men.   Where are the exiles to go?   The Free States are too crowded and Canada too cold for them.   Can we not offer them an asylum in Jamaica and other colonies?   They are the cream, the best of their race; for it is by long-continued industry and economy that they have been enabled to purchase their freedom, and joyfully will they seize the hand of deliverance which Great Britain holds out to them. We only want additional labour; give us that and we shall very soon cultivate our own cotton.

Another consequence of the triumph of the Free State party in November will be hailed with satisfaction by every tax-paying Englishman. We shall no longer be compelled to keep up expensive fleets on the coast of Africa and in the Mexican Gulf, for the new Government at Washington will reverse the foreign policy of the Slave power, and render the Slave-trade impossible.*

* Were our Government to encourage the cultivation of cotton along the western coast of Africa, any future anxiety as to supplies of that staple would be obviated, and we should have done, for ever, with the trade in African slaves. Cotton is indigenous to that continent, and labourers may be numbered by millions. Let it be shown to the chiefs, who now carry on continual wars for the sole purpose of replenishing their coffers by the sale of their prisoners, that the cultivation of the cotton-plant would be immeasurably more remunerative, and they would quickly desist from killing the goose that lays the golden eggs. Our present policy with regard to the Slave-trade is simply ridiculous; we enhance the value of the shipments which evade our cruisers, and thus offer an inducement for the continuance of the traffic.

CONCLUSION.

But a far nobler result—the noblest result of all—remains. By the voice of her new President, from the steps of the Capitol, America will declare she has done with Slavery, she recognizes not its existence, she denies all property in man. In that happy era now dawning, when Slavery shall be declared " sectional "—when human bondage, encircled and confined by ever-increasing Free States, shall decay and die —when Washington, the seat of government, shall emulate Washington, the patriot, and desire some general scheme of manumission for every oppressed child of Adam—when the glorious truth of the Declaration of Independence, " All men are born *free* and *equal*," shall no longer be " a mere glittering generality "—in that bright future which God is now hastening, the poor fettered " chattel " will burst his chains and stand erect—A MAN !

THE END.

www.ingramcontent.com/pod-product-compliance
Lightning Source LLC
Chambersburg PA
CBHW020114030726
47498CB00006B/2093